HELP ME! / AYUDAME!

Please Explain My Benefits!

Por Favor Explicame mis Beneficios

DELL HOUSEWRIGHT

TRAFFORD

USA ▪ Canada ▪ UK ▪ Ireland

Note for Librarians: A cataloguing record for this book is available from Library and Archives Canada at www.collectionscanada.ca/amicus/index-e.html

Aviso a Bibliotecarios: La catalogación bibliográfica de este libro se encuentra en la base de datos de la Biblioteca y Archivos del Canadá. Estos datos se pueden obtener a través de la siguiente página web: www.collectionscanada.ca/amicus/index-e.html

ISBN 1-4120-8957-3

PUBLISHING™

Offices in Canada, USA, Ireland and UK/
Oficinas en Estados Unidos, Canadá, Reino Unido e Irlanda

EDITORIAL

Book sales for North America and international /
Venta de libros en América del Norte y al extranjero:
Trafford Publishing/ Editorial Trafford, 6E–2333 Government St.,
Victoria, BC V8T 4P4 CANADA
phone/ Teléfono: 250 383 6864 (toll-free/ llamadas sin cargo: 1 888 232 4444)
fax 250 383 6804; email to orders@trafford.com / pedidos@trafford.com
Book sales in Europe: / Venta de libros en Europa
Trafford Publishing (UK) Limited, 9 Park End Street, 2nd Floor
Oxford, UK OX1 1HH UNITED KINGDOM
phone/ Teléfono: +44 (0)1865 722 113 (local rate/tarifa local 0845 230 9601)
facsimile/ Fax: +44 (0)1865 722 868; info.uk@trafford.com/ pedidos.ru@trafford.com
Order online at: / Pedidos por Internet:
trafford.com/06-0713

10 9 8 7 6 5 4 3 2 1

Contents

Contenido

Help Me!

Please Explain My Benefits!

DELL HOUSEWRIGHT

*A Guide in English and Spanish
For Those Trying to Understand
Their Employee Benefits*

Acknowledgements and Thanks

This book is dedicated to my friends.
They edited my ideas,
Offered ideas and support,
And always encouraged me to complete the
project.

Bill Thurin
Christie Howard
Linda Bryant
Deborah Thornburg
Patricia Daniels
Elizabeth Gonzales

_____

Disclaimer

The purpose of this book is not to provide legal, tax, or accounting advice. My purpose is to provide the information and perspective you need to make sound decisions. Every effort has been made to ensure the accuracy of the information provided. The author accepts no liability for any inaccuracies, errors, or omissions. Read the brochures that are provided with your employer sponsored plan. For a more complete explanation of pre-taxing and flexible reimbursement plans, you can go to the **IRS Web site (www.irs.com). Another source of information is IRS Publication 503,** Dependent Child Credit. The IRS gives more information than you ever wanted to know.

Introduction

For more then fifteen years I have worked with companies and helped explain to their employees what company benefits were being offered. I also assisted employees in enrolling in the plans best suited for each individual. It was a rare occasion when I attended an enrollment meeting and the benefits offered by the company were adequately understood by the employees. Sometimes there was a group meeting where the employees were given a booklet and told to make choices. Other times, the booklet was handed out without any meeting of any kind, and employees were told to make their benefit choices on a web site, over the phone, or by checking boxes on a preprinted form.

It has always been up to the employee to make sense of what benefits are being offered and what meets their needs. When I met individually with employees, I learned that they did not know the differences in the medical and dental plans being offered. They did not know the differences between group and individual products. Long-term and short-term disability plans merged in their minds, and voluntary benefits were a total mystery. Generally, the employee would choose what he needed for the new plan year based on what he had last year, or on what a friend had or how attractive the plan sounded.

Most of the questions employees asked me were related to the construction of the plan. "What will this do for me?" "How does it work if something happens to me?" "How do I choose a doctor?" "Where do I go?" "Do I really need this?"

To find their own answers, the employee had to read through the plan, ask the HR person, or ask the representative of the insurance company. This brings up the biggest question of all, one that was often unasked. "Can I trust you to help me choose what is right for me?"

Everyone the employee turns to for help has their own agenda. The HR person may want you to have what you need, but she is usually not an insurance agent and does not have all the answers. The representatives of the insurance companies may have your best interests at heart, but they are there to explain how well *their product* is the one that meets your needs. Your friends, co-workers, and your family will advise you on what they have found to be best for them, though it may not be the best for you. We all need a little help.

This book is not intended to make you an expert on health benefits but to teach you enough about the various choices available to enable you to make informed and intelligent decisions. Enjoy the chapters, get the basic plans in your head, and then keep this book in your library to refresh your memory before each enrollment.

Chapter 1

Why Benefits?

Employers have different motivations for providing insurance benefits to employees. The most common is for retention. The employer who is concerned about retention wants to have an *Employee Benefit Plan* that is equal to or slightly better than the plan offered by his competition. Benefits are a significant part of the employee paycheck. When you are looking for employment, you should not be solely motivated by the pay per hour. You need to know what else is in the package. You should be asking the following questions. "What is the medical and dental coverage?" "Is there life insurance for me and my family?" "What about disability if I am injured?" "What else does this company offer?" "What does the company pay and what do I pay?"

For many years, it was common for larger corporations to pay for everything. The benefit booklet was half an inch thick and the employee just took everything. As health benefits become more expensive and profit margins began to dwindle, this all-inclusive type of plan has become hard to find. To maintain an acceptable level of benefits, employers have had to shift costs to the employees. One of the most common reasons given when a company faces bankruptcy is the high costs of employee health benefits.

Some employers have truly altruistic reasons for providing benefits. They really want their employees to have the best benefits the company can afford. Such employers may not have the best plans, but these companies are always looking for extra benefits to offer. They believe that employees who are secure in knowing they and their families are protected will be happier and more productive. These employers will provide what they can and offer supplemental benefits for those that want them and are willing to pay the additional premiums.

Other employers are less generous. Some employers grudgingly provide only what may be legally required. These employers will have many excuses, but not many benefits. They believe that they pay a good wage and provide a place to work...and that should be enough!

Most employers will fall somewhere between these two extremes. In most cases, you will find benefits that encourage retention. The quality and quantity of the benefits are thus a direct result of how management believes they will affect retention. Each organization will also consider other factors. One employer may not like life insurance, another sees no need for cancer insurance, and a third may believe it is the employees' responsibility to get these benefits on their own. It is always going to be the responsibility of the employee to be aware of benefits. The smartest employees are their own best advocates.

Chapter 2

Medical Insurance

M edical insurance is probably the most important, and least understood, of all employee benefits. A common belief among employees is that they don't need to worry about medical insurance because at the time they are considering choices, they are not sick nor injured. And besides, they believe when they get sick or injured, the plan, whatever it is the company offers, will take care of them!

Health insurance has a language of its own. Here we will cover the most popular choices and attempt to demystify the language and choices. But before that, here is a small glossary to help with the rest of this chapter.

HMO:	Health Maintenance Organization
DMO:	Dental Maintenance Organization,

	also called Prepaid Dental Plan or HMO Dental
PPO:	Preferred Provider Organization (consists of a large group of doctors)
EPO:	Exclusive Provider Organization (similar to the PPO Medical or Dental Network except there are no out of network benefits)
Indemnity:	All doctors and dentists may participate for a predetermined fee for service.
Self Insured:	Employer becomes the insurance company and assumes all responsibility for paying for the services outlined in the coverage.
Network:	A group of doctors, clinics and hospitals that have agreed to the rules and rates of a medical plan.
Co-pay:	The amount the patient pays at time of service
UCR:	Usual and Customary, An amount determined by surveying the local area to discover what is commonly charged by doctors, clinics, and hospitals.

HMO

The HMO (Health Maintenance Organization) plan was started to help maintain the health of large groups of people. The plan design was to encourage the patient to visit the doctor at the first symptom of distress so the problem could be cured before it became worse.

Early detection equaled early cure which meant less cost for all involved.

When you pick an HMO plan you select a Primary Care Physician, (PCP); sometimes called a gatekeeper. This is your doctor. You will see him first and he will refer you to specialists as needed. There are exceptions that allow you to pick a Gynecologist without a referral but you need to ask if this exception is allowed in your plan. Each member of your family can usually pick a separate PCP. You are allowed periodically to change PCPs.

Each visit will require a co-payment; sometimes called a co-pay. This is your share of the cost of service. Typical co-pays today range from five to fifty dollars. The most common are $15, $20, and $25. After you have made this payment, there are usually no additional charges for this visit including any lab work or x-rays. If a referral to a specialist is required, another co-pay will be charged when you visit that specialist. Visits to the emergency room will have higher co-pays, usually waived if admitted to the hospital. Some plans require separate co-pays on admission to the hospital. These co-pays are disclosed in the plan description you receive when you choose a plan. Be sure to look for these costs!

Normally the specialist where you are referred is a member of or affiliated with your PCP's physician group. This method of control tends to keep costs down and usually the premium is less costly. The PCP is also associated with specific hospitals which limit where you can go for hospital treatment. In a large doctor group with lab facilities, etc. it is usually easier and faster to get referrals and tests completed because it is all done under the same roof. The extreme of this is the closed model HMO where even the hospital facilities are associated with the doctor group. An example of this closed staff model is Kaiser Permanente. Most facilities you might need such as doctors offices, specialists, labs, and hospitals are located in one location. However, unlike the open model HMO, you cannot change to another group of doctors not affiliated with the closed model.

The open model HMO will have several different physician groups from which to choose. For example under a plan like Pacific Care's HMO you will choose a doctor of your choice and then you will get the hospital, clinic, and specialists where he is associated.

With all HMO plans you must stay in the network to use the plan. Only in a real emergency will the plan pay for services outside the network. Be aware of how your plan works if you are traveling and need care.

PPO

The PPO plan entails a deductible and a percentage paid by the insured. The deductible is an amount the insured pays out of pocket before the plan starts paying benefits. The Plan has a maximum amount of out of pocket expenses and then the insurance company pay 100%. It does not require a PCP or gatekeeper. You may choose any doctor in the network. Many plans have an office visit co-payment and a prescription co-payment that is not counted toward the deductible and the out of pocket expense limits.

The normal PPO plan works like this: See your doctor and get services and pay 100% out of your pocket until the deductible is met. You then are responsible for a percentage (usually 10%, 20% or 30%) of all costs until the out of pocket maximum is met in addition to your deductible. Once that out of pocket maximum is met you usually have no more payments for that year no matter how much you use the plan.

PPO plans that have the physician co-pay and drug co-pay work exactly the same way except your physician and drug co-pays are totally outside your deductible and out of pocket maximums. This allows you the freedom to get normal office visits, physical exams, and normal medications without having to satisfy your deductible.

The PPO plan also allows you to visit a doctor outside the primary care network. Since these doctors, clinics, and hospitals have not agreed to specific costs of services, you normally will have to pay the difference. The out of network is designed exactly like the in network except the deductible and percentages that you pay are usually higher and the out of pocket maximum is usually higher. Also, any costs over the fee schedule of the PPO or the UCR schedule of the PPO are your responsibility to either pay or negotiate to a lower amount.

Typical plans will have the patient paying 30%, 40%, or 50% of the usual and customary fees and the insurance carrier will pay the other 70%, 60%, or 50%. A problem could occur if the out of network doctor chosen charges higher then the usual and customary fees or the fee schedule established by your carrier. Here is an example. The usual and customary fee for a medical procedure is set at $500. This doctor chooses to charge $700. In this case the carrier will pay $350 (70%

of $500.00) and you are responsible for the balance due of $350.00 plus the $200 extra charged by the doctor. The $200 extra charged is also outside your out of pocket maximum and will make your total medical costs for the year higher.

Be very careful when going outside a Medical or Dental PPO network and know your costs before proceeding. Remember, inside the network the costs are established and you have deductibles and percentages spelled out that will always be honored but only if you stay in the network.

EPO

The EPO (Exclusive Provider Organization) plan is designed like the PPO except there is no option to go out of the network. Typical plans will have the split costs formula where the patient pays 20% and the carrier pays 80%. When you go out of network there is no coverage. Be sure to check the rules for handling emergency calls if traveling out of your network area.

Indemnity

Indemnity plans offer the most freedom of choice. The patient is allowed to go to any doctor and the cost of services paid by the carrier is going to be a percentage of the usual and customary fees established for that area. There is usually a deductible from $250 to $1000 per year per person with a cap for families. Some new plans will have an even higher deductible to lower the premium cost. The deductible is the amount the insured has to pay before the insurance starts paying.

After the deductible has been satisfied the plan will pay or reimburse you at a percentage of the usual and customary prices for the area. The percentage paid by the insurance company is usually 80 or 90%. Read over the description of the plan to be aware of the deductibles, percentage paid, and any other conditions required. Remember, in an indemnity plan you have no network so the charges from the physician can be very different in each office because there is no network controlling the charges.

Self-Insured and Partially Self -Insured Health plans

Self-Insured Health plans are becoming more popular among large employers, school districts, and other government entities. These employers collect premium from the employees and form a pool of money to pay the claims of employees. Usually the employer will have a third party administrator (TPA) to administer the plan. The employer can also contract with an Insurance company to act as TPA. These plans will most often work as a PPO plan. But they can be HMO or Indemnity plans.

COBRA

The Consolidated Omnibus Budget Reconciliation Act (COBRA) is a federal law that has an important effect on medical insurance. When you have a qualifying event such as reduction of hours to part-time from full-time, or termination of employment, this law allows the employee to continue health coverage for up to 36 months. The group policy must be in force with 20 or more employees covered on more then 50% of the business days of the previous calendar year. Here are the qualifying events and coverage time allowed.

Qualifying Events	Beneficiary	Coverage
Termination	Employee	18 months
Reduced hours	Spouse	18 months
	Dependent child	18 months
Employee entitled to Medicare	Spouse	36 months
	Dependent child	36 months
Divorce or legal separation	Spouse	36 months
	Dependent child	36 months
Death of covered employee	Spouse	36 months
	Dependent child	36 months
Loss of dependent child status	Dependent child	36 months

If coverage is requested under COBRA the insured is required to pay the full premium including the amount previously paid by the employer. The employer can also charge two percent of the total premium for administration costs.

Cal-COBRA

Cal-COBRA is for California residents and is similar to COBRA. This plan extends COBRA to 36 months for the qualifying events of termination and reduced hours. Cal-COBRA applies to group policies with 2-19 employees covered. If you experience a qualifying event which causes the loss of health benefits, be sure to ask about COBRA and Cal-COBRA coverage. If not a California resident, inquire of the Human Resource Department if a similar plan is in effect in your state.

HIPAA

In 1996 the Health Insurance Portability and Accountability Act (HIPAA) was passed. This plan has a couple of features all employees should know. The act protects individuals that have recently lost their employer sponsored group health coverage. All insurance companies that offer individual health coverage must offer you health coverage even if there are pre-existing health conditions. This means you may not be declined health coverage for medical reasons. To qualify for this you must meet the following conditions.

1. The last health care coverage you had must have been in an employer sponsored group health plan, including COBRA for at least 18 months.
2. All available COBRA or Cal-COBRA (for California) has been used or the plan is terminated entirely by the employer.
3. You are not eligible for another group health plan or Medicare, (medi-Cal in California).
4. You did not lose your coverage because you did not pay premiums.

If this situation occurs, and you are eligible, there is a 63 day window to file an application for a guaranteed issue HIPAA health insurance policy. You will need to obtain a Certificate of Creditable Coverage from your former carrier. This Certificate can be used as proof of your 18 months coverage.

The Accountability portion of the HIPAA Act is designed to guide health care providers and insurance providers in their handling of your personal information. The guidelines and regulations are much more stringent then before the Act was passed and you have more control of how your personal information can be used. During enrollments you are sometimes asked to sign a HIPAA form. The main purpose of this form is to give permission to doctors and other providers to discuss your condition if there is a claim.

Healthy Families Program.

There is another program offered in most states that allows parents to obtain health, dental and vision coverage for children. In California it is called The Healthy Families Program. It is for parents that have too much income to qualify for public assistance, but not enough to pay for comprehensive major medical for their children. For the California website and more information go to www.healthyfamilies.ca.gov . Most states have a similar program.

Chapter 3

Dental Insurance

Dental insurance is probably the most misunderstood of the basic health insurance plans. Most people believe their plan is bad because it costs too much and pays too little. This is probably the most shared misconception I hear about dental insurance. Before we look at the types of plans lets take a look at the basics of how dental insurance works. In order to get the most benefit from any plan it is important to understand how it works.

Our fictional company, Tom's Dental Insurance, is formed to sell group dental insurance. The owners want to provide a benefit plan they can sell at a low price that will help their customers and make a profit for the company. It is important they make this profit so they can stay in business. In its simplest form the business plan requires the customers to pay a monthly premium for the plan. This premium is then used to pay dentists, company overhead and profit.

Dave's Tool Shop purchases a dental plan for their 100 employees. The plan costs 5 dollars per week per employee for a total of $26,000 per year. Fifty percent of the employees use the plan at an average pay out of $500 for a total expense to the dental plan of $25,000. This leaves Tom's Dental Insurance with $1000 for the year to pay all overhead and contribute to profit. This example shows only half the employees using the plan.... and only $500 in benefit! This plan can expect to have a price increase at renewal. For the individual it should be easy to see that paying $240 per year for $500 in benefits every year is not a reasonable expectation.

Dental plans typically have a higher percentage of employees that use the plan as compared with other benefit programs. This means there is less of the premium paid that is available to pay benefits. Thus the maximum payout amounts are lower, typically $1000, $1500, or $2000 per month. In many cases, dental plans are voluntary. Employees that only require annual cleaning often do not take the insurance and reduce the pool of available premiums needed to cover those requiring more work. Taking a couple of minutes to examine the cost effectiveness of the plan is well worth the time.

With that said, let's take a look at the typical plans available. The four most popular plans are DMO, PPO, EPO, and Indemnity. All the plans have some common traits. The plans collect premium from the customer and pay the dental providers for services. All plans negotiate with the dental providers to secure discounts for services in return for access to the plan's customers. The differences are in what and how the plan pays.

DMO

The DMO is the Dental Maintenance Organization plan. It is very similar to the HMO plan used for medical coverage. The dental providers accepting this plan are paid a specific amount each month by the dental plan for each client assigned to that dental office. In return for this the dental providers have agreed to provide some services for no additional cost, and have agreed to specific discounted costs (co-pays) for other services. Each person choosing this plan will have to choose a particular dentist or dental office that accepts this plan. This is then your primary dentist. The intention is you will stay with this dentist for the period of the plan and he is responsible for your dental work.

The primary dentist is chosen from a panel of dentists that agree to co-payments for all their services. These co-payments are listed in the coverage agreement provided by the dental insurance carrier. When extensive work is needed a written summary of procedures and charges should be requested before agreeing to the work. This list can be checked against the coverage agreement. If there are any discrepancies, always ask questions before the procedures are done. If the procedure is not on the list from the insurer you can insist on a similar procedure that is on the list and will be covered at the agreed rate.

The primary dentist will refer you to specialists as necessary. Most plans will allow you to change dental providers as often as monthly if you are not satisfied with your choice. There is usually no limit to the number of procedures you can have performed because each procedure has its own co-payment. If you go to a dentist outside the network you do not have coverage.

PPO

The PPO dental network is organized very similar to the PPO medical network. There is usually a deductible and then a percentage the patient has to pay. The plans are usually set up in three tiers; preventative, basic and major.

The preventative tier includes normal cleaning, x-rays, and examinations. This is usually allowed once or twice per year with no or little charge. It is sometimes referred to as a 100% benefit. In most plans the deductible (typically $50 or $100 does not apply to preventive procedures.

The basic tier includes most extractions, fillings, and most normal less expensive services. Sometimes root canal work and periodontal services are covered in basic and in other plans will be covered as major. The deductible must be satisfied first and then a percentage is applied. Typically the patient will pay 10%, 20%, or 30% with the insurance paying the remainder.

The major tier includes the more expensive procedures such as dentures, partials and surgical procedures. Major works just like basic in which the deductible must first be paid then a percentage is applied. The patient can expect to pay 40%, 50%, or 60% and the insurance carrier will pay the remainder.

PPO Dental plans always have a maximum amount the insurance carrier will pay each year for each person insured on the plan. That amount is typically $1000 to $2500.

When you go out of network the PPO dental plan works exactly like the PPO medical plan. Your deductible and co-payment percentage will usually be higher. You will also be responsible to negotiate a rate equal to the UCR or Fee schedule or you will have to pay the difference. Many PPO plans have lower maximums they will pay out of network. With major work in any plan you should get a written cost of services the dentist intends to provide along with your cost before you start so there are neither surprises nor misunderstandings.

EPO

The EPO dental plan works like the PPO dental plan except there are no benefits out of network. For this reason the EPO plan premiums are usually less expensive. This could be an advantage considering the PPO and EPO networks are usually very large compared to the HMO networks so there is a better chance of finding the dentist you prefer.

Indemnity

Indemnity dental plans work just like PPO plans except there is no network to control prices. You can choose any dentist who is willing to accept the insurance plan. It is most important here that you communicate with your dentist what your share of costs will be. If not you could be very unpleasantly surprised!

Chapter 4

Vision Insurance

There are two main types of Vision insurance. One is an insurance plan that pays a portion of expenses. The other is discounted service through a network of Doctors and eye clinics. The insurance plan will typically be more expensive and pay more benefits. The discounted service plan will have negotiated within the network for specific prices for specific services. If glasses are needed, either plan will usually save you money. If glasses are not needed and you just want to get the free exam, you may be better off not paying the premium and using that money to pay for the annual exam. Always look at the cost of premium vs. the services you could receive.

The typical PPO Vision Plan has either a free eye exam inside its panel or a specific deductible toward the eye exam, usually $10 to $25 for the exam.

There is usually an allowance for frames equal to a certain quality of frames. Those are usually no cost to the patient. The more expensive frames require you to pay the difference.

The same is true for lenses. Certain types of lenses are covered and extras are usually paid for by the patient. Most plans also cover a specific amount toward contact lenses.

There are always time limitations for each service. Typically you are allowed and exam either annually or every two years. Lenses are allowed either annually or every two years, and frames are allowed either annually or every two years. A typical plan would allow an eye exam annually, lenses annually, and frames every two years. The shorter time frames make for more expensive plans.

There are some plans that only cover eyewear and not the exam. This can be a good choice if your medical plan allows for an annual eye exam.

Chapter 5

Pre-Tax vs. Post-Tax

Prior to the mid-1970s, most large companies that provided health insurance benefits paid the entire cost. That was the era when the rising costs of health care were just becoming a major issue and companies were starting to shift some of the costs to the employee. In 1978, IRS regulations took effect. These regulations allowed the employee who was paying a portion of his or her premium for health coverage through payroll deduction to have these funds deducted from his or her pay before taxes, allowing the employee to use gross dollars to pay for certain benefits. This program reduced the payroll amount and created a tax savings to both employee and employer. Over the years, the idea of pre-taxing benefits has become the norm, and the initial program grew to include flexible spending plans for medical expenses and dependent day care. We will take a quick look at these later in the chapter.

Pre-taxing premiums can be used for the employee's portion of medical, dental, and vision plans, as well as many supplemental plans like cancer insurance, critical illness, and hospital income. Some companies advocate pre-taxing the premiums for disability plans, and some companies advocate *not* pre-taxing disability, critical illness, and some other lump payment plans. This difference in allowable plans derives from varying interpretations of the IRS code and the fact that we really seldom know what the IRS will do next year. With life insurance, for example, you are not allowed to pre-tax the premiums. For more information about what the IRS allows and disallows, you can go to the IRS Web site (www.irs.gov) and read about Section 125 and all of its addendums.

To better understand the benefit of pre-taxing insurance benefits, we need to do some simple arithmetic. Start with a man who has an income of $30,000 per year. He is in a 20 percent tax bracket and pays $200 per month for health benefits. The following table shows the effect on this man's take-home pay when benefits are paid with post-tax or pre-tax dollars.

	Post-Tax		Pre-Tax
Monthly Income	2500		2500
Tax @ 20%	-500		
Pre-Tax Benefit Costs	-200		-200
Net Pay	1800	Net Pay	2300
		Tax @ 20%	-460
Take-Home Pay	1800		1840

As we can see, the post-tax column shows the taxes and benefits subtracted from the gross pay. The employee's take-home pay is $1800. In the pre-tax column, we can see that the benefits are subtracted first, then taxes are taken from the lower amount. This yields a lower tax bill and provides an increase of $40 per month in take-home pay. This difference is where the term "tax savings" was coined. The benefit of spending pre-tax dollars for benefits creates tax savings and increased take-home income.

At this point, it is important to emphasize that the savings derived from pre-taxing benefits come from *tax savings*. If you are not paying taxes, there is no benefit. Someone with family income of $20,000, for example, and four dependents, will probably not have a tax bill. It would still be a good idea, however, to pre-tax medical, dental, and vision plans because you will receive a small saving on each paycheck throughout the year. Medical reimbursement plans and dependent care plans have no tax-saving value.

You also need to look at the long-term effect of pre-taxing. A cautionary note is usually included in pre-tax plans to warn you that pre-taxing benefits will reduce your gross income and could reduce your eventual Social Security benefits. While this is true, however, the effective loss is far outweighed by the gain over time.

Another area of concern is the pre-taxing of disability premiums. Unlike the other benefits discussed here, disability benefits become taxable income when the premiums are paid pre-tax. Your employer has to pay FICA taxes on the benefits you receive, which causes a reduction in your benefit and can cause problems with your employer. The amount saved by pre-taxing is good if you never have a claim, but when a claim is filed, the savings are rapidly eaten up. Why do some disability salespeople recommend pre-taxing? They are trained to show tax savings as a way to reduce the costs of current benefits. And since most of us will not need to file for disability, the savings will reduce your costs.

You need to watch lump sum payment cancer, critical illness, and medical bridge plans. At the time this book is published, the benefits paid under these plans are still nontaxable, but under rules the IRS has used in similar cases, this status could change at any time. Be sure you get the latest IRS ruling from the insurance company representative at the time of sale. If they do not have that information available, then it is more prudent to *not* pre-tax.

I recommend that you *never pre-tax* disability plans. I recommend that you *do pre-tax* medical, dental, vision, and most other voluntary products.

Flexible Spending Accounts

A flexible spending account is another way to save tax dollars. The account works by allowing you to set aside dollars in a separate account, the funds to be spent later on medical expenses and dependent care costs. The savings are realized by having the employer reduce the employee's gross pay *before taxes are calculated* by the amounts to be placed in these accounts. This program gives the employee a lower gross income to be taxed and results in higher spendable income.

Medical Reimbursement Accounts

Medical reimbursement plans are the most frequently used flexible spending accounts. A medical reimbursement plan allows the employee to set aside pre-tax dollars to pay approved out-of-pocket expenses, such as co-pays and deductibles, prescriptions, chiropractic, vision care, and some over-the-counter drugs. There is a list of approved expenses with each account. Be sure you have access to this list before you choose this plan. The amount you can select is a yearly total and cannot be changed without a change in family status (marriage, divorce, birth or death of a family member) or a major change of employment status for the employee or spouse. The IRS sets the boundaries, but interpretation gives individual plans some leeway. Any funds in this account at the end of the plan year may be forfeited, so it is important that you be conservative in picking the amount that is set aside. The employer sets the minimum and maximum amounts that employees can choose to set aside.

The mechanics of how a medical reimbursement account actually works can be confusing to the person considering using the account for the first time. Although not all plans work exactly alike, there are many consistencies. Let's go through a typical plan.

Our employee chooses this plan and selects $1200 as the amount she wants to set aside for the plan year. She picked this amount by estimating what she would spend out of pocket for approved expenses during the year. She knows she may spend more and could spend less, so $1200 is a calculated estimate.

Co-pays and deductibles	$ 500
Dental	500
Vision	200
Prescriptions	200
Total	$1400

Another consideration is the "use-it-or-lose-it" rule. The IRS requirement is that any amount left over at the end of the plan year is forfeited. *Note that this is not a company rule. It is an IRS regulation.* Your estimate, therefore, should be conservative. It is OK if you don't have enough in the account. If that is the case, you just pay as you would normally pay with your normal paycheck. But if you have too much in the account, you may lose it.

The $1200 is deducted from the employee's paycheck and evenly divided over the year. If there are twenty-four pay periods, $50 is deducted from each check. Most employers have a third plan administrator (TPA) to manage these accounts and disburse the funds. Employees can access the funds up to the maximum set aside from day one of the plan. If the employee in our example spends the whole $1200 in January and the TPA reimburses the entire $1200, there is no money left in the account for expenses during the rest of the plan year. Confusion arises because this is a *savings account*; it is *not* insurance. Deductions and deposits to the account continue for the rest of the plan year to replace the amount withdrawn in January.

To access her $1200, the employee must have an approved expense. A pair of prescription glasses would be an approved expense. If the out-of-pocket expense is $120, the employee can pay it and get receipt from the optometrist. She then submits the receipt to the TPA and is reimbursed for the $120. Most TPAs will send the reimbursement check within forty-eight hours of receiving a claim. (Counting mail time, this could mean you will get your check in a week to ten days.) The $120 is subtracted from the employee's account, leaving $1080 waiting for the next claim.

Variations on the plan allow bills or receipts to be submitted with the claim. Some allow you to fax your claim to the TPA (eliminating mail time), and the TPA may also offer direct deposit to your bank account if you have a debit card and used it at the point of sale. All of these methods are designed to help get your reimbursement claim handled faster.

Reimbursement accounts are easy to use if you understand how they collect and hold your money and how they give it back to you. The tax savings can be substantial for those with allowed expenses. The "use-it-or-lose-it" rule is only a problem if your planning is inadequate or your estimate is not conservative.

Dependent Care Accounts

Dependent care accounts assist with childcare expenses so the employee and/or spouse can go to work. Dependent care can be daycare, after-school expenses for children under age thirteen, or care for an adult dependent. The employee can set aside up to $5000 per year for the dependent care account (or $2500 per year if spouses are filing separate tax returns). This plan has the same "use-it-or-lose-it" rule, so it is important to be both conservative and accurate when estimating projected costs. If the employee's gross family income is $25,000 or less, the tax credit for dependent care may be a better option. There is a formula to use that shows which is the better option. Most companies that administer this program provide a worksheet at enrollment to determine if the dependent care plan or the tax credit is better. If your family income is less then $25,000 annually or you have more then two children in dependent care, be sure to use the worksheet provided.

If you choose this plan, you designate an amount to be set aside. This amount is deducted from you gross paycheck over the year. Unlike the medical reimbursement account, you can use only the amount in your account. You pay the dependent care expenses as usual, and after the services have been provided, you submit your claim form and receipts to the TPA, who will send you the reimbursement check.

Chapter 6

Disability Insurance

Disability insurance (DI) is probably the most misunderstood of all the insurance plans available in a benefits package. In this chapter I will try to define the different types of DI and give you enough information to choose the plan that is right for you.

DI is often called "paycheck protection," "payroll replacement," or by a similar term that ties the benefit to payroll. The assumption is made that if you become disabled, you won't have a paycheck. The benefits of this plan allow you continue to take care of your financial responsibilities during the period you are disabled and not drawing a paycheck.

The typical short-term disability (sometimes called STD) plan pays a percentage of your income from 25 to 60 percent after you are off work from zero to thirty days for a period of three months to two years. As you can see, there is a lot of room for variation among plans.

A typical long-term disability (sometimes called LTD) plan will pay a percentage of your income from 25 to 70 percent after you are off work from thirty days to one year and will pay from five years to age sixty-five or longer. Again, there is a lot of room for variation.

Because of the great variation in plans, there is also a great variation in the price you pay for the individual plans. But price is not the only factor. To choose the plan that right for you, you must examine the whole plan. Here is a list of the parts of a DI plan.

> Premium
> Age
> Elimination period
> Amount of benefit payment
> Length of benefit payment
> Pre-existing conditions rule
> What constitutes disability?
> What conditions result in not being covered?

This is not to say you don't need to look at the premium. Look at the cost of the plan on an annual basis. Plan A, for example, costs you $50 per month, or $600 per year, and pays you a benefit of $500 per month after you have been out of work for two weeks for one year. You would have to be out of work for seven weeks to collect as much as you paid in. This is where you look at your job and your lifestyle and make an educated guess of your own probability of using DI. A young person who is not very active might be better off just saving a couple months of income for emergencies, whereas no one who rides a motorcycle should be without accident coverage.

Your age also affects your premium. Most plans have increased prices with increased age. I don't believe your risk is any greater, but I know that as we get older, our reactions may be a little slower and our injuries take longer to heal. It is wise to always check the age brackets. Also find out at what age the plan stops paying benefits. Most plans cover you from age eighteen to sixty-five, though some will go higher if you are still working.

The elimination period is the amount of time, usually expressed in days, after your disability starts before your coverage begins. Short-term plans typically range from zero to thirty days, though some plans will go as high as sixty or ninety days. This is the period when you are on your own; the plan is not paying you any benefits. How do you choose? The simple test question is, "How long can I go without my paycheck?"

When considering a DI plan, take into account all other possible sources of income. Rhode Island, New Jersey, New York, Hawaii, California, and Puerto Rico offer a state disability plan, (SDI, to be discussed below). You may also have sick pay, vacation pay, employer-paid salary continuation plans, savings, or even kind-hearted relatives who will help you. The longer you can go on your own before the benefit starts to pay, the lower the premium you will pay.

Long-term DI typically has an elimination period of three, six, or twelve 12 months. It is designed to take over after short-term disability and other sources of income expire.

The amount of your benefit payment is usually expressed as a percentage of your normal gross paycheck and can range from twenty-five to seventy percent. Short-term disability plans typically do not coordinate with other sources of income, including other DI plans, so these benefits are paid on top of SDI and any other income. The percentages are set to attempt to get the benefit close to your take-home pay without going over it. Since California's SDI plan typically pays 55 percent of your gross paycheck, a twenty-five to 40 percent supplemental DI plan is most commonly offered. In states without an SDI program the percentage is usually sixty to eighty percent. Insurance companies and employers tend to watch this percentage closely so they do not give you any incentive to not return to work.

It is important to remember that DI plans are affected by pre-taxing plans. If your company pre-taxes the premium, your benefit becomes taxable income. Be sure to keep this in mind when considering how much benefit you need. Most plans will allow you to take less than the maximum allowable benefit. For instance, if 40 percent of your income is $2000, but because of other resources you can get by with $1200, taking the lower amount will save you premium dollars. But if the plan is a pre-tax plan and your benefit is taxed you may need to choose $1500 to get the same take-home pay.

Different plans also have different durations of benefit payments. The duration is the period of time the plan will pay you when you are off work. The typical short-term DI plan ranges from three months to two years, usually six or twelve months. If you suffer a broken leg and are off work for seven months, the six-month plan will pay the benefit for six of your seven months off. The twelve-month plan will pay the full seven months, but the premium for the twelve-month plan will be higher.

Long-term DI is designed to start after short-term DI has expired and typically pays for five years, to age sixty-five, or to retirement. Long-term DI plans are typically paid by your employer and have a longer elimination period, which may be six months or one year. Most plans will also coordinate with other disability coverage you may have. Coordination means the DI company will not pay more than 100 percent of the stated benefit. When you file a claim, the insurance company will ask if you have other coverage. They will then reduce their coverage to *coordinate* with your other coverage.

This can become confusing when your employer offers a long-term plan that pays benefits after an elimination period of six months. He may also offer a voluntary SDI plan, so you can choose coverage that will pay a benefit for six or twelve months. The short-term plan claims the benefit does not coordinate with any other coverage and pays on top of any other income you may receive. This is probably true. Most SDI plans are non-coordinating.

The coordination comes from the long-term plan. In the example below you can see how this works. Your long-term plan (LTD) offers a benefit of 70 percent and your short-term plan (STD) offers a benefit of 60 percent. The disability period is eighteen months. The short-term plan pays 60 percent for the first year, and then stops. After six months, when you file for long-term disability, the insurance company will ask if there is other coverage. Since the short-term plan is paying

60 percent for the first six months of the long-term coverage period, the long-term plan will pay only 10 percent, which is the difference between the 60 percent the short-term plan pays and the 70 percent offered by the long-term plan. When the short-term plan stops paying after one year, then the long-term plan starts paying at the 70 percent rate. Look at the following time line.

TIME	0 months	6 months	12 months	18 months
STD @ 60%	----------------------------			
LTD @ 10%		--------		
LTD @ 70%			---------	

You will receive 60 percent for the first six months from your short-term plan. You will receive 70 percent for the next six months, with your short-term plan still paying 60 percent and long-term paying 10 percent. You will receive 70 percent for your final six months on disability, with the long-term plan paying the full 70 percent.

When you have multiple plans, it is very important that you understand the coordination policies of the different insurance companies. If anyone tells you they do not need to explain coordination, or for any other reason you decide not to inform the long-term plan insurance company about your short-term policy, consider this cautionary note. When a claim form is completed, one of the statements you sign is that the form is filled out completely and truthfully to the best of your knowledge. If there is a *no* in a box where there should be a *yes*, and the insurance company finds out, they could consider this fraud and refuse to honor the claim. Some LTD plans *do not* coordinate with some STD plans. Be sure you understand the coordination policy of both companies involved.

Pre-existing conditions are a part of all disability plans. Typical wording is something like the following:

> Benefits will not be paid for the first twelve months after issue date for any condition that was diagnosed, treated, or discussed by or with any medical professional during the twelve months prior to the issue date.

Each plan has its own way of wording this clause. Some plans will have longer or shorter periods, and some will make the pre-existing condition a permanent bar. The intent is that the insurance company does not have to pay for an accident or illness that occurred before you were covered. This can also apply to maternity claims. Some plans will not pay maternity benefits if the birth is within the first nine months after policy issue date. Other plans require you to not have been diagnosed before the application date. Be sure you read and understand any pre-existing condition clauses before you sign the application.

Sometimes a DI policy will be issued as *guaranteed issue.* This means you are guaranteed the policy will be issued if you meet the terms of the guarantee. This usually eliminates all or most of the health questions on the application, but usually does not eliminate the pre-existing conditions clause. When you are told the policy is guaranteed issue, you must still check for pre-existing conditions.

Every DI plan has a definition that explains what constitutes disability. This is the condition you must satisfy in order for the insurance company to pay benefits for your claim. A typical definition is "the inability to perform the normal duties of one's job." There are many variations of the definition, most of which require the certification of an M.D. or other qualified medical practitioner to be submitted with the claim form.

Every plan also has a section that explains *what is not covered*. These are usually called "exclusions." Exclusions are always in the policy itself, but they are also usually listed on the brochure. Look in the fine print. You will usually find a statement similar to this:

> This policy will not pay if the claim is a result of war or civil disturbance, the commission of an illegal act, participation in any form of organized racing or exhibition of speed, piloting or being a crew member in a private aircraft, or hang gliding, parachuting, or bungee jumping.

Exclusions can be more or less detailed. Some plans exclude high school sports if you cover dependents. Different insurance companies have different concerns about what is dangerous, so read this section of the policy or brochure carefully.

State Disability Insurance

Consider a quick note for those with a state disability

plan. This is a plan that pays a disability benefit if you are sick or injured off the job. The California plan pays fifty-five percent of your gross pay after you are off seven days and will continue to pay up to one year. If you are in one of the six states with this type program you need to be aware these benefits are considered when you are allowed to choose a voluntary disability plan. That is why with most disability insurance companies in these states, you cannot get more then a forty percent benefit.

Chapter 7

Life Insurance

Many companies provide a modest amount of life insurance to their employees, usually a flat benefit of $10,000, $20,000, or more. Some companies offer a multiple of salary, like one or two times your annual salary. More companies are recognizing that employees want more life insurance and are starting to offer additional voluntary options.

The life insurance benefit, which is paid out upon the death of the named insured (usually you), is purchased to take care of your survivors. While there are many approaches that address how much life insurance is right for you, I offer a simple, conservative way to examine your needs.

Everyone needs at least enough assets to cover final expenses so they are not a financial drain on their relatives, friends, or the state. These days, if you do not have $10,000 in net assets, you need at least that much insurance. Most insurance paid for by an employer is not portable, which means if you change jobs or quit, you lose that benefit. I recommend that you carry this minimum $10,000 in addition to any temporary insurance your employer may be carrying. For a single person with no responsibilities, this may be all you need.

For a person who is married and/or has a family, the rules change. Everyone has dreams and desires for their life and the future of their families. The means to those dreams and desires coming to fruitation is the income you produce while you are alive. When that income stops, then your life insurance becomes the means. What is it going to take to realize your family's dreams?

To understand life insurance we need to look at how it is constructed. In this book, we are looking only at life insurance as it is commonly provided in employee benefits. The three types you will most often see are *term, universal,* and *whole life.* A simple way to differentiate the three types is by looking at the cash value. Term life insurance has no cash value. Think of it like car insurance—no crash, no cash. Universal life insurance is a more permanent type of insurance where you pay a higher premium and the insurance company pays interest on the premium at a floating rate that reflects the market. Whole life insurance is a permanent insurance where you pay a higher premium and the insurance company pays a fixed rate on the premium.

When insurance companies decide to sell life insurance, there are a few basics they look at. We need to remember these companies are in business to make a profit. A company's mission statement may list other goals, but without profit they do not stay in business. To make a profit, they must bring in more money through premiums and investments than they pay out in claims and operating expenses. As consumers, we must remember this basic concept as we study pricing.

Premium rates are generally based on age, smoking status, and a range of other health questions, plus sometimes gender. Most life insurance plans offered through employee benefit plans are unisex plans, so we will not deal with gender as a pricing issue. The best rates will go to the younger person who is a non-smoker and can answer the health questions in a positive way. This is because history has shown that this person will live longer and thus pay more premiums than the older person, the smoker, or someone with health problems.

One of the advantages of getting your life insurance through your company benefit plan is the concept of guaranteed issue. This means you will have a guarantee that the policy will be issued if you meet the conditions of the guarantee. Many plans offer guaranteed issue or modified guaranteed issue on the first opportunity you have to purchase the life insurance. This is as a new hire employee or when the employer first introduces the plan. You will still be rated by age and smoker status, but the health questions will be simplified and sometimes waived completely. This is a marketing strategy. The insurance company's goal is to sell more policies. The increased volume of sales will cover the potential loss caused by a few policy-buyers who get covered but would not be accepted if full health questions were asked. This is good for the insurance company. It is also good for the employee who takes advantage of this opportunity.

Term Life Insurance

Term is the simplest form of life insurance. The basic term plan is a specific amount of insurance benefit that pays out on the death of the named insured and is in effect for a specific term of time. A ten-year term plan for $100,000 will be good for ten years. At the end of ten years, that policy is finished. You do not get any money back. Your benefit is having the use of the life insurance policy during the 10 year term at a lower cost. At the end of the term you may have the right to renew for another period at a higher rate commensurate with you current age.

If an employer offers a basic life insurance plan for all employees, it is generally a group term plan. The term is the period of your employment, and these plans are usually not portable, so when your employment ends so does your insurance. There are exceptions, so be sure to check your benefits guide or ask your benefits representative.

Most of these plans are convertible. Do not confuse *convertible* with *portable*. Portable means you can continue the plan, as it is written, after you end your term of employment and at the same price as you or your employer were paying when you were employed. Convertible means you can continue the plan after you end your term of employment, but you must convert the policy to another form, such as whole life, and pay a much higher premium. This is usually a good idea only if there are health issues preventing your obtaining other life insurance and the convertibility clause does not require new health underwriting.

The most common form of voluntary group term insurance is the five year term. The premium for this plan is rated in five-year bands, usually twenty, twenty-five, thirty, thirty-five, etc. This means the premium you pay is based on your age when you buy or when the insurance is issued. The year after your age passes one of the bands; your premium will increase to the next level and stay there for five years. Until you reach age forty, the increases are minimal, but at forty-five years and older, the increases in premium can be significant. If you have this type of plan, be aware of the increases each time you pass to the next age band.

Term insurance is a good decision if you are under fifty, in good health, need over $100,000 in coverage, and only need the coverage for a specific period of time. Keep this in mind: one type of life insurance is not better than another. You need to determine how much life insurance you need, why you need it, and what you can afford to invest. Later I will give some examples of clients with different needs and the preferred way to satisfy those needs.

Universal Life Insurance

Universal life insurance is often called "permanent" insurance. Unlike term insurance, universal will stay in force as long as the cost of insurance is paid. The cost of insurance is the amount the insurance company charges to keep the insurance in force. The premium for universal life insurance consists of the cost of insurance plus an additional amount that, when invested by the insurance company, will provide for the increased cost of insurance as you grow older. This additional amount creates the cash value of the policy. The cash value allows you to pay a level premium for the life of the policy. Remember, however, that the cost of insurance goes up every year as you grow older, unlike term insurance, where the premium rises every year or five years or whatever the age band requires, and the policy stops at the end of the term. With universal life insurance, the amount of premium is constant and the policy continues. The extra amount paid into the premium is what pays for this to happen.

If universal is more expensive, what is the value in buying it? Universal will be permanent and portable. You will be able to keep the policy until you die, even if you change employment. Most insurance companies will allow you to keep your payroll-deducted universal life plan, at the same price, if you change jobs or retire. This is a valuable feature, especially if you develop health issues as you get older. In most cases, the price will stay constant, and in most plans, unless there is a serious decline in interest rates, your premium is designed to make the policy last until you are ninety-five (in some cases, 100) years old.

For a younger person looking at the long term, the universal plan may be the best value. See the example in the table, below. Unlike individual policies, most plans sold in the employee benefit market have unisex rates. Therefore, the premium rates will be the same for a man or a woman. The main factors are going to be smoker status and age. A person who is purchasing a $100,000 life policy at age twenty-five and who is a non-smoker will pay the following premiums over thirty years.

Type	$ per week	Years of Premium	Total Paid	Cash Value
Term	$ 4.60	10	$ 2,392.00	$ -
Term	$ 6.38	10	$ 3,317.00	$ -
Term	$ 16.06	10	$ 12,526.00	$ -
Total		30	$ 18,235.00	$ -
Universal	$ 12.87	30	$ 20,077.00	$ 34,729.00

Term life insurance is cheaper, even with the increased rates required as the employee ages. However, remember that the policy terminates when you reach age fifty-five and there is no further coverage. That is, you spent $19,431 with no other return except the feeling of security realized by knowing you were covered for thirty years. With universal, you spend almost $2000 more over thirty years, but you have a continuing policy at the same rate and cash value at the guaranteed rate of four percent for over $34,000. The results will be different if you are a different age or a smoker. The older you are when you start, the less the return. However, the price still stays constant and the policy remains permanent.

Keep in mind that these are sample rates given to help you understand what questions you need to ask about different policies. Neither is better than the other! The plans have different purposes. Some people actually buy term insurance and invest the difference in cost of premium for a better return over time. Of the thousands of people I have talked to on this subject, I have met few who actually did the investing. I prefer to believe the main value of universal is its permanence. When you reach an age where the term premium becomes unaffordable, there is still universal continuing at the same premium you were paying when you first signed the application. Term, therefore is for a specific period of time, whereas Universal is permanent for life.

Here are some common riders offered with universal life insurance. There are others, and not all plans offer these. If there is a rider and you don't understand it, be sure to ask.

Accelerated death

This rider gives you the option to receive a percentage of the death benefit, usually 50 to 75 percent, if you are diagnosed with a terminal illness and it is expected you will die within one year.

Accidental death

This rider is additional term insurance that pays if your death is caused by an accident. It usually doubles your benefit amount.

Additional term for spouse or children

This rider allows the addition of insurance for a family member to be a part of your policy. Amounts are usually limited, but the price is low.

Waiver of premium

This rider waives all monthly deductions if total disability occurs before you reach age sixty-five. Some plans require permanent disability, whereas others will waive deductions while you are disabled. You can continue payments after the disability ends.

Increased benefit

This rider allows the insurance company to increase your insurance benefit in the amount that one or two dollars per week will buy for five or ten years without any evidence of insurability. This gives you an easy way to increase your benefit over time with a slight increase each year, instead of paying a higher premium in the beginning.

Chapter 8

Supplemental Health Insurance

Supplemental health coverage has become popular as a way to help with the expenses related to a specific illness or injury. Health insurance costs continue to rise, and cuts in benefits and/or increases in deductibles and co-pays are being used to hold back the price increases. This causes gaps that have to be paid out of your pocket. Another popular feature of most supplemental policies is that the benefits are paid in cash, and you can use this money for anything. For example, your health insurance may cover the doctor and hospital charges, but it will do nothing to cover your rent or childcare expenses.

In addition to assisting with co-pays and deductibles, supplemental coverage can be used to help with caretakers, and household expenses. It can supplement your disability income or help you meet any other expected or unexpected expenses. The most popular supplemental benefits are accident plans, cancer insurance, critical illness coverage, hospital income, and medical bridge plans.

Accident Plans

Accident plans, probably the most popular supplemental benefits, come in many different formats with different riders. Some have short-term disability riders that will pay a monthly DI benefit on top of the accident benefit. Some plans offer spouse and child coverage. Others offer an optional benefit for disability or hospital confinement due to illness. Because this is a universal favorite, it is important to be sure you understand which features your company-sponsored plan offers.

This plan is popular with employees who are concerned about the costs associated with accidental injuries. Medical plans are seldom all-inclusive and do not cover all expenses. When you are injured and cannot work you still have expenses.

The basic accident plan is designed to offer a predetermined benefit for injuries caused by accidents. This money is usually in addition to any other benefit paid by the health insurance or other plan. It is paid to you (not a doctor or hospital) and can be used for any purpose. A typical plan may offer benefit payments for the following needs::

Ambulance
Appliances

Blood
Burns
Dislocation
Emergency room treatment
Eye injury
Fractures
Knee cartilage
Cuts

Most plans offer benefit payments for more than the ones I list below, but this list gives you an idea of how the plan works. Say you have been in a motorcycle accident and suffers two breaks in you right leg. This plan would pay as follows:

Ambulance	$100
Emergency room	$150
Appliance (brace)	$100
Broken leg bone (1)	$1200
Broken leg bone (2)	$600
Hospital Admission	$750
Hospital Confinement (10 days)	$2000
Total	$4500

You will receive an additional $4500 to assist with co-pays, deductibles, or any other expenses that may occur.

Typical exclusions are war, flying as a pilot or crew member, professional sports, participation in a felony crime, being intoxication, and racing. If the child plan is selected, some plans exclude high school football and other sports. Be sure to check exclusions on the plan offered.

Cancer Insurance

Cancer insurance is offered because of the high risk of cancer today. The American Cancer Society claims men have a one in two lifetime risk of developing cancer, and women have a risk of one in three. The ACS also claims the five year survival rate of people having had screening for cancer is 80 percent. They also claim in the 2000 edition of *Cancer Facts and Figures* that if all Americans participated in cancer screenings, this rate could increase to 95 percent. (footnote Cancer facts and Figures, American Cancer Society, 2000)

Using the American Cancer Society figures, direct costs covered by most major medical plans equal only 35 percent. The 65 percent indirect costs that you pay include loss of income, travel to treatment centers, lodging, meals, co-pays and deductibles, second opinions, and seeking treatment outside your network.

Looking at the ACS statistics, it is no surprise additional insurance for cancer has become so popular. Many different companies offer cancer insurance plans, most of which are either a single payment benefit or an indemnity plan that pays benefits depending on what occurs.

Both types of cancer insurance generally have similar definitions of cancer and limitations. All insurance companies have their own wording, so be sure to check the definitions of the plan sponsored by your employer. Cancer is usually defined as a disease characterized by the uncontrolled and abnormal growth and spread of invasive malignant cells. This could include melanoma, Hodgkin's disease, and leukemia. The cancer has to be diagnosed clinically or pathologically.

Both types of cancer insurance also usually include a wellness benefit. This is a benefit that pays once per year for you to take a cancer screening test. The amount paid varies, but is usually between $50 and $150. The tests covered by different companies are not all the same, but usually include mammography, PSA for prostate cancer, chest x-ray, biopsy for skin cancer, colonoscopy, hemocult stool analysis, and flexible sigmoidoscopy. Different policies may cover different cancer screening tests, so be sure to check your policy to determine which tests are covered. Nonmalignant skin cancer is usually covered at a lower rate than other malignant cancers.

There is often a waiting period between policy issue and policy effective dates. This means if the cancer is detected during the waiting period, (usually thirty days, but could be longer), it will not be covered. To be safe, always wait for the waiting period to end before taking any screening tests. Another common limitation is the pre-existing condition clause, which usually states that if you have already had cancer or have skin cancer, you may not be eligible for coverage. Different plans will have different limitations. Some plans say "never had," whereas others will accept you if you are considered in remission or cured for ten years, though for others it may be five years, and even less for skin cancer. It is very important to check which rule your employer-sponsored plan applies.

The single payment benefit is a plan that allows you to choose a single payment, usually between $5,000 and $50,000, to be paid on diagnosis. The cost of this plan is usually based on age, smoker status, and the amount chosen as the benefit.

The indemnity plan is more complex and can include treatment benefits, in-patient benefits, transportation and lodging benefits, extended care benefits, and others. Most plans have a brochure that spells out the individual benefits. Here are some examples of the benefits offered.

Hospital confinement	$200 per day
Attending physician visit	$20 per day
Ambulance	$150 per trip
Radiation/chemotherapy	$10,000 per year
Experimental treatment	$10,000 per year

This money can be used for any purpose. Always check your brochure to see what your plan pays.

Critical Illness Insurance

Critical illness insurance, sometimes called survivor's insurance, is designed for people who get one of the named critical illnesses and survive it. These illnesses are known for the high expense of treatment and time lost from work, which usually puts the survivor in dire financial straits.

A typical plan covers heart attack, stroke, kidney failure, major organ transplant, and coronary artery bypass surgery, though some plans cover more illnesses, some fewer. Check your employer's plan to see what conditions or illnesses are covered. The typical plan allows a choice of benefit levels from $5000 to $50,000, to be paid on initial diagnosis. These plans usually have a waiting period and exclusions for pre-existing conditions.

Hospital Income Plans

Hospital income plans are designed to cover co-pays, deductibles, and other expenses that may occur when you are hospitalized. The typical plan pays a flat amount per day for every day you are a hospital patient. The rate is often one and one-half to two times the base rate for days spent in intensive care. The value of this plan is that it fills in any gaps in your other medical plan. For example, if your other medical plan is a PPO with an 80/20 payout and the average cost per day in the hospital is $1000, then a $200 dollar per day plan will pay the 20 percent of your responsibility.

Medical Bridge Plans

Medical bridge plans are designed to fill the initial deductible gap found in many medical insurance plans. They cut expenses and fight increases in premiums with increased deductibles and co-pays. The hospital income plan helps with the co-pays and deductibles; the medical bridge plan does the same, but in a different way. This plan is usually available in benefit levels from $500 to $5,000, to be paid on admission to a hospital. If your medical plan has a co-pay or deductible of $500, $1,000, or more on admission, this plan will recover your out-of-pocket expenses regardless of the medical plan you have, but it is much more useful if your medical plan has gaps that need to be bridged.

Long -Term Care plans

Long-term care plans are not usually included in

employer benefit plans and are usually sold individually. Some employers offer a payroll slot when unions and associations sponsor these plans. Some life insurance policies have also started offering riders that can help pay long-term care expenses.

Long term care (LTC) refers to nursing home care and (sometimes) home health care expenses. Most companies use the seven activities of daily living criteria—dressing, eating, transferring, using the toilet, bathing, transporting ones self and taking medication— to determine when you qualify for payment. You must not be able to perform two or three of these activities on your own to qualify, though different plans have different requirements.

The typical plan will be set up to pay a set benefit for each month of long-term care, up to a maximum in time or dollars. A plan might offer $4000 per month for thirty-six months or $4000 per month for life, up to a maximum of $240,000. The wide range of features and benefits makes this an individualized plan.

The long-term care plan usually be found in a employee benefit plan is a rider attached to a universal life insurance plan. As a rider, it is easier to understand, so it is more popular in groups. With this plan, an employee may purchase a $100,000 universal life policy. A feature of the policy, or an attached rider, will state that if long-term care is needed before death, the policy benefit (or a portion of the benefit) may be used to pay those expenses. Typically, this means that the policy will pay out $100,000 divided by twenty-five months, which equals $4000 per month for twenty-five months. Some variations on this may allow $2000 per month for fifty months, and for an additional premium the twenty-five months can be extended to fifty months at the $4000 level. Any amount of the benefit not used for long-term care will be available for the death benefit. The exception to this is if the extension was purchased, the left-over amount would only apply to the original benefit amount.

Group Legal Plans

Although they are quite popular in employer benefit plans, most group legal plans are not insurance, but plans designed to cut the costs of legal services. They work like an HMO health plan. You pay a monthly fee, pick a lawyer or lawyer's office, and receive legal services for low or no co-payments. There are two basic types: access and comprehensive. An access plan costs about $150 per year and usually provides a simple will and phone access to an attorney for advice and simple legal services.

A comprehensive plan costs about $300 per year and covers negotiations, trusts, deeds, or contracts. Some plans also provide legal counsel in criminal cases up to a cost limit, after which the attorney will continue to represent you at a reduced rate. The lawyer does not usually handle any case involving you and your employer, nor do they take on a case already in progress. The greatest benefit is the easy access to an attorney for advice. Sometimes this can prevent an issue from getting out on hand and resulting in a large, expensive lawsuit.

There are many plans available. Be sure to read the brochure. Be aware of the scope of the services and any other additional costs beyond your premium.

Chapter 9

So What Do I Do?

The big question is how much does the insurance cost and why is it so expensive. Newspaper and magazine articles have sacrificed forests of trees exploring and answering these questions. The bigger question is how you can have a direct effect on your health care costs? First, don't smoke, drink, overeat, undereat, or eat the wrong stuff. Do nothing dangerous and exercise regularly. Don't hang around sick people, get checkups every year, and get your shots. Practice moderation. Avoid obvious activities that are known to cause illness and try to live a full healthy life. Most important, remember that no matter how well we live our lives, there will still be times we will need medical care.

So, you ask, what plan is right for me? With company benefit plans, you do not always have a choice of which plan to choose. With smaller companies, you may have only one or two choices. Before you look at benefits, determine what kind of coverage you already have. Are you single with few responsibilities? Do you have a family that needs to be protected? Are you nearing retirement and already have the assets needed for a comfortable life? Or are you just starting out and still living on a shoe string? Everyone is different. Here are three basic guidelines I have developed over the years. They may not be perfect for everyone, but they are a good place to start.

1. Don't be a burden on someone else. Everyone needs medical insurance. There is no way to guarantee that you won't get sick or injured. Someone always has to pay the bills.
2. Everyone needs to be able to pay their own burial expenses. Everyone dies. We just don't know when. Someone will have to pay the bills.
3. If you have a family, you need to provide for their welfare if you are hurt or sick and can't work, or if you die and leave them without an income.

A good argument can be made to justify the necessity of each plan in your employer-sponsored benefit plan. That is why they are there. To decide what plans are right for you, I suggest an approach that considers risk and cost. You try to cover the greatest risk for the least cost. History shows that the greatest risk is that you will get sick, be hurt, or die. These choices create healthcare expenses and can stop your income. I suggest that your priority should be medical insurance, the disability insurance, and then life insurance.

Consider your age, family health history, your own health history. How active are you? Do you drive a lot? Are you a smoker? Do you drink? What risks do you believe you have? How much of the total cost will your health insurance pay? , These considerations can lead you to the supplemental plan that is right for you. No two people are alike. You need to pick the best coverage that works for you at the best price you can afford.

HELP ME! *Please explain my benefits!*

————————————

AYUDAME!

Por Favor Explicame mis Beneficios

D E L L   H O U S E W R I G H T

*Una guia en ingles y espanol, para aquellos
que tratan de entender sus beneficios de
empleados.*

Reconocimiento
y
Gracias

Este libro esta dedicado a mis amigos
Ellos analizaron mis ideas
ofrecieron idas y me respaldaron
y siempre me animaron a terminar el projecto.

Bill Thurin
Christie Howard
Linda Bryant
Deborah Thornburg
Patricia Daniels
Elizabeth Gonzales

———————————

DESDEN

El proposito de este libro no es para proveer taxes legales o advertencia de contabilidad, mi proposito es proveer la informacion y perspectiva para que ustedes puedan hacer decisions razonables. Se ha hecho todo lo possible para asegurar la exactitude de la informacion proporcionada. El autor acepta cero liablilidad por cualquier inexactitud, errores e omiciones. Lea la informacion que es proveida por el plan que su empleo patrocina.

Para una explicacion mas completa de pre-taxes y planes reembolsados, isted puede ir a **la web de IRS (www.irs.com) otro lugar de informacion es IRS publication 503**, Deoendent child credit, El IRS da mas informacion de la que usted quiere saber.

Introduccion

Por mas de quince anos yo he trabajado con companias y he ayudado a explicar a sus empleados que beneficios eran ofrecidos por su compania. Yo tambien asisti a los empleados a inscribirse en el plan que era mas conveniente para esa persona en individual. Era una ocacion muy rara cuando yo atendia una junta y los empleados entendian adecuadamente los beneficios de los empleados ofrecidos por la compania, Algunas veces habia una junta en donde se les daba un libreto a el grupo en donde se les decia que escogieran. Otras veces el libreto era entregado nin reunion de ningun tipo y se les decia a los empleados que escogieran en una website, por telefono o marcando cajas en una formea anteriormente imprentada.

Siempre ha sido requerido de el empleado que haga sentido de que beneficio son ofrecidos y cuales se adhieren a sus necesidades. Cuando yo conocia empleados individualmente, yo aprendi que ellos no sabian la diferencia entre el plan medico y dental que les ofrecian. Ellos tampoco sabian la diferencia entre grupo y productos individuales. Largo y corto plazo, planes

---

de disabilidad aparecian en sus mentes y beneficios voluntarios eran un misterio total Generalmente el empleado escogia lo qie el necesitaba para el plan de el ano basado el lo que tenia el ano anterior, o en lo que una amistad tenia, o en que atractivo se veia el plan.

La mayoria de las preguntas que los empleados me hacian eran relacionadas a la construccion de el plan "Que va a hacer esto por mi?" "como funciona si algo me pasa?" "como escojo a un doctor?" "Adonde voy?" "yo necesito esto en realidad?"

Para encontrar su propia respuesta el empleado teni que leer el plan, preguntarle a la persona de HR o preguntarle a el representante de la compania de seguros.

Esto hacia que resultara una pregunta mucho mayor, la cual casi nunca preguntaban "puedo yo confiar en que usted me ayude a escoger lo major para mi ?".

Todo aquel empleado que pida ayuda tiene su propia agenda. la persona de HR puede querer que obtengas lo que necesitas, pero ellos no son usualmente agents de aseguranza y no tienen todas las respuestas. Los representantes de las companias de seguro puede que tengan tu major interes pero ellos estan alli para explicar que tan bien (su producto cubre tus necesidades) Tus amigos, companeros de trabajo y tu familia te advertiran en lo que ha funcionado mejor para ellos, aunque no sea lo major para ti. Todos necesitamos ayuda.

Este libro no esta intencionado a hacerte un experto en beneficios de salud, pero si intentar ensenarte lo suficiente acerca de las distiintas oportunidades ofrecidas. Para que puedas hacer decisions informativas y inteligentes. Disfruta los capitulos, obtiene los planes basicos y conservalos en tu mente y entonces mantenga este libro en su biblioteca pare que lo ayude a refrescar su mente antes de cada nueva inscripcion.

Capitulo 1

Por que Beneficios

Los empleos tienen diferentes motivos por el cual proveen beneficios medicos a sus empleados, El mas comun es por retencion El empleo que se preocupa por retener a sus empleados quiere tener un plan de beneficios para el empleado que es igual o un poco mejor que el plan que es ofrecido por la competicion. Los beneficios son una parte significante de el cheque de el empleado. Ciuando usted esta buscando empleo no va a ser motivado solo por el pago por hora, usted va a querer saber que mas hay en el paquete. Usted va a estar preguntando las siguintes preguntas "Cual es la covertura medica y dental?" "hay aseguranza pra mi y mi familia?" "que de disability si yo estoy asegurado?" "Que mas ofrece la compania?" "que es lo que la compania paga?" y "que es lo que yo pago?"

Por muchos anos era comun que las companias grandes pagaran todo. El libro de beneficios era media pulgada de grueso y el empleado recibia todo. A medida que los beneficios medicos se pusieron mas caros y ganancias empezaron a tambalear este tipo de plan inncluso se ha hecho dificil de encontrar. Para mantener un nivel aceptable de beneficios los empleos han tenido que transferir gastos a los empleados. Una de las razones mas comun que es dada es que cuando una compania enfrenta banca rota es por el alto costo de beneficios de salud para el empleado.

Algunos empleos tienen en verdad sinceras razones para proveer beneficios, ellos en realidad quieren que sus empleados tengan los mejores beneficios que la compania pueda ofrecierles. Estos empleos puede que no tengan el major plan pero estas companias siempre estan buscando por beneficios extra para ofrecerlos. Ellos creen que empleados que estan seguros sabiendo que ellos y sus familias son protegidos van a ser felices y mas productivos, estos empleos proveeran lo que ellos puedan y ofreceran servicios suplementarios para aquellos que los quieran , y estan dispestos a pagar los pagos adicionales.

Otros empleos son menos generosos algunos empleos duramente provienen lo requerido por la ley. Estos empleos van a tener muchas excusas, pero no muchos beneficios. Ellos creen que pagan un buen salarioy provienen un lugar de trabajo y que eso es suficiente.

La mayoria de los empleos caen entre estos dos extremos y en la mayoria de los casos usted va a encontrar beneficios que son atractivos y provocan retenerlos. la cualidad y cantidad de los beneficios son entonces un resultado directo de come el manteniemiento va a afectar la retencion de estos. Cada organizacion tambien va a considerer otros doctores. A un empleo puede que no le guste el seguro de vida, otro no va a ver necesidad para seguro de cancer. Y un tercero puede creer que obtener estos beneficios es la responsabilidad de el empleado. Siempre va a ser la responsabilidad de el empleado esta al tanto de estos beneficios, el empleado inteligente es el advocado mas inteligente de si mismo.

Capítulo 2

SEGURO MEDICO

Seguro medico es probablemente el mas importante y el menos entendido de todos los beneficios. Una creencia comun entre empleados es que no necesitan preocuparse de seguro medico porque en el momento que estan considerando opciones no estan enfermos o heridos. Es mas ellos creen que cuando se enfermen o se lastimen el plan cualquiera que sea el que la compania halla escogido va a cubrirlos y cuidar de ellos. Seguros de salud tienen su propia lengua Aqui vamos a cubrir las opciones mas populares y tratar de decifrar el language y opciones. Pero antes de esto aqui esta un pequeno diccionario para ayudar con el resto de el libroy este capitulo.

HMO	Organizacion de mantenimiento de salud

DMO	Organizacion de mantenimiento dental tambien llamada plan dental prepagado o HMO dental
PPO	Organizacion de proveedores preferida consiste de un grupo grande de doctores
EPO	Organizacion exclusiva de proveedores similar a PPO medico o dental Excepto que no hay beneficios fuera de esa cadena
INDEMNITY	Todos los doctores o dentistas pueden participar por un pago pre- determinado por el servicio
Asegurado por si mismo	El empleo se convierte en la compania de seguros y assume la responsabilidad para pagar los servicios que estan sub-rayados en lo que cubren
Cadena	Grupo de doctores, cinicas y hospitals que estan de acuerdo con las reglas y cobros de un plan medico
Co-pago	La cantidad el paciente paga en el momento de servicio
UCR	Usual y acostumbrado, una cantidad intermedida por medio de encuestas en el area local para descubrir que es comunmente cobrado por doctores, clinicas y hospitales.

HMO

El HMO (organizacion de mantenimiento de salud) plan fue empezado para ayudar a mantener la salud de grandes grupos de personas. El diseno de este plan era para entusiasmar a el paciente a visitor a el doctor en la primera senal de malestar asi el problema podia ser curado antes de empeorar. Temprana deteccion significaba cura la cual significaba menos costo para todos los involucrados.

Cuando usted escoge un plan HMO usted selecciona a un doctor primario, (PCP)

Algunas veces llamado (guardarejas) este es su doctor. Usted lo vera a el primero y el lo referira a un especialista si es necesario. Hay algunas excepcioness que permiten que escoja a un ginecologo sin referencia. Pero usted necesita preguntar si esta excepcion esta incluida en su plan. Cada miembro de su familia usualmente puede escoger un PCP separado usted es permitido cambiar su PCP periodicamente

Cada visita require un co-pago algunas veces llamados pr-pagos este es su parte por el costo de los servicios

Los co-pagos tipicos hoy dia varian de cinco a cincuenta dolares. Los mas comunes son de $15, $20 y $25. Despues que haya hecho el pago usualmente no hay cargos adicionales por esta visita incluyendo trabajos de laboratorios o rayos x. Si una referencia a un especialista es requerida otro co-pago va a ser cobrado cuando usted visite a ese especialista. Visitas a emergencia van a tener cobros mas alto de co-pago ususalmente cancelados si usted es admitido a el hospital, estos co-pagos estan escritos en la descripcion de el plan que usted recibe cuando usted escoge un plan. Asegurese de buscar estos precios

Normalmente el especialista que usted es referido es un miembro o afiliado con su PCP grupo medico. Este metodo de control mantiene los costos bajos y usualmente los pagos mas bajos.

El PCP tambien es asociado con hospitales en especifico lo cual limita a donde usted puede ir para tratamiento en un hospital . En un grupo grande de medicos con facilidades de laboratorios etc. es usualmente mas facil y rapido obtener una referencia y completar los examenes pues todo es echo bajo el mismo techo. El extreme de esto es es el modelo cerrado HMO en el cual hasta las facilidades de el hospital son asociadas con el grupo de doctores. Un ejemplo de esto es Kaiser Permanente Casi todas las facilidades que usted requiera como oficinas de doctores, especialistas, laboratorioy hospitals estan localizados en un local. Sin embargo no como el HMO plan abierto, usted no puede cambiarse a otro grupo de doctores que no estan afiliados. Con todos los planes HMO isted tiene que quedarse en la cadena para usar el plan. Solamente en una emergencia el plan pagara por servicios afuera de la cadena, este conciente de como su plan funciona, si usted esta viajando y necesita ayuda medica.

PPO

El plan contiene un deducible y un porcentage pagado por el asegurado. El deducible es un costo que el asegurado paga antes que el plan comienze a pagar beneficios. El plan tiene un costo maximo que paga por gastos y despues la compania de seguros paga el

100%. Este no require PCP y guardarejas. Usted puede escoger cualquier doctor que used quiera en la cadena. Muchos planes tienen un co-pago de visita a la oficna y un co-pago por prescripciones o recetas que no es contado hacia su deducible y el dinero que usted paga fuera de su limite de gastos.

El plan PPO normal trabaja asi. Vea a su doctor y obtenga servicios y pague 100% fuera de su bolsillo hasta que el deducible es alcanzado. usted entonces es responsable por un porcentage (usualmente 10%, 20%, o 30%) de todos los costos hasta que el maximo de fuera de su bolsillo sea alcanzado junto con su deducible. Una vez que el fuera de bolsillo maximo es alcanzado usted no tiene mas pagos que hacer por ese ano no importa cuanto usted use el plan.

PPO planes que tienen el co-pago medico y co-pago de prescripciones trabajan exactamente de la misma manera excepto que el co-pago medico y de prescripciones estan totalmente fuera de su deducible y fuera de el maximo. Esto le permite la libertad de obtener visitas a la oficina normales, examenes medicos, y medicamentos normales sin tener que satisfacer a un deductible.

Tambien , cualquier costo sobre la lista de pagos de el PPO o el UCR lista de pagos de el PPO son su responsabilidad para pagar o negociar un precio mas bajo.Planes tipicos tienen a el paciente pagando 30%, 40%, o 50% de los cobros normales y el encargado de aseguranza paga el otro 70%,60% o 50%.

Un problema puede ocurrir si la cadena de doctores de afuera escogen pagos mas altos de lo normal y usualmente acostumbrado o el itinerario de cobros establecido por su encargado de aseguranza. Aqui esta un ejemplo El cobro usual y acostumbrado por un procedimiento medico esta establecido a $500. Se este doctor decide cobrar $700 en este caso el encargado pagaria $350[70%de $500] y usted seria responsible por el balancede $350 mas los $200 extra cobrados por el doctor . Los $200 extra cobrados son tambien de el maximo cobrado fuera de su bolsillo y va a hacer sus costos medicos anuales mas altos.

Tenga mucho cuidado cuando se salga de una cadena medica o dental de PPO y sepa sus costos antes de proceder. Recuerde, adentro de la cadena el costo esta establecido y usted tiene deductibles y porcentages escritos detalladamente que siempre van a ser garantizados si usted se queda em la cadena.

EPO

El plan EPO (organizacion proveedora exclusiva) esta disenado come el PPO excepto aqui no hay opciones para salirse de la cadena. Planes tipicos tendran la formula de costos divididos adonde el paciente paga 20% y el cargador paga 80%. Cuando usted se sale de la cadena alli no hay cobertura. Asegurese de revisaer las reglas para cobertura si usted sale fuera de la area de su cadena

Indemnidad

Planes de indemnidad ofrecen las opciones mas liberals. El paciente es permitido ir a cualquier doctor y el costo de servicios pagados por el cargador es un percentage de los cobros usuales y acostumbrados ya establecidos para esa area. Aqui solamente hay un deducible de $250 a $1000 por ano por persona por familia. Algunos planes nuevos tienen un deducible aun mas alto para bajar el costo de el pago. El deducible es el costo el asegurado tiene que pagar antes que la aseguranza empieze a pagar. Despues que el deducible ha sido satisfecho el plan pagara o regresara un porcentage de los precios usuales y acostumbrados por esa area. El porcentage pagado por la compania de aseguranza es usalmente 80 o90%. Lea la descripcion de el plan para estar al tanto de sus deductibles, porcentages pagados y otras condiciones requeridas. Recuerde, en un plan de indeminazion usted no tiene cadena asi que los cobros de el medico o dentista pueden ser muy diferentes en cada oficina pues no hay cadena que controle los cobros.

Planes de aseguranza medica propia y parcialmente – asegurado

Planes de Aseguranza propia se estan haciendo mas popular entre los empleos grandes, distritos escolares y otras entidades governamentales. Estos empleados coleccionan un pago de sus empleados y hacen una bolsa de dinero para pagar los cargos de empleados. Usualmente el empleo tiene a una tercera persona administradora (TPA) que administra el plan. El empleo puede tambien contratar con una compania de seguros para que actue como TPA. Estos planes casi siempre trabajan como el tipo de plan PPO.Pero tambien pueden ser HMO o Plan de indemmidad.

COBRA

El plan consolidado omnibus de reconcilizacion budget act (cobra) es una ley federal que tiene un efecto importante en aseguranza medica. Cuando usted tiene un evento calificador cini una reduccion de horas a tiempo medio de tiempo completo o terminacion de empleo. Esta ley permite a el empleado continuar su covertura medica hasta 36 meses. La poliza de el grupo debe estar enforzada con 20 0 mas empleados cubiertos en mas de 50%de los dias de negocios de el ano previo. Aqui estan los eventos y tiempo permitidos para coverturra.

Eventos para calificar	Beneficiario	Covertura
Terminacion	empleado	18meses
Horas reducidas	esposa	18 meses
	Hijo(a) dependiente	18 meses
Empleado que le		
Corresponde medicare	esposa	36 meses
	Hijo(a) dependiente	36 meses
Divorcio o separacion		
Legal	esposa	36 meses
	Hijo(a) dependiente	36 meses
Muerte de empleado		
Que esta cubierto	esposa	36 meses
	Dependiente	36 meses
Perdida de estatus		
De el dependiente		36 meses

Si cubrimiento es requerido bajo cobra el asegurado es requerido a pagar el costo total de pagos incluyendo el costo previamente pagado por el empleo. El empleo puedo tambien cobrar dos por ciento de el pago total por costos de administracion.

Cal-Cobra

Cal-cobra es para residents de California y es similar a cobra este plan extiende cobra por 36 meses por los eventos de qualificacion de terminos y horas reducidas. Cal cobra se aplica a polizas de grupo con 2-19 empleados que son cubiertos.

Si a usted le sucede un evento que califica el cual causa la perdida de beneficios de salud, asegurese de preguntar acerca de covertura cobra y cal-cobra. Si no es residente de California pregunte en el departamento de los recursos humanos si hay un plan similar en efecto en su estado.

HIPAA

En 1996 El acto de aseguranza de salud, portabilidad y contabilidad (hipaa) fue pasado.

ESte plan tiene unas cosas que todo empleado debe saber. El acto protégé individuos que recientemente han perdido la covertura de grupo de su empleo. Aun si hay condiciones de salud que pre existian. Esto quiere decir que usted no puede ser negado covertura medica por razones medicas. Para calificar usted debe cumplir las siguientes condiciones.

1 la ultima covertura medica que usted tuvo tiene que haber sido un plan con un grupo respaldado por un empleado , incluyendo a cobra por lo menos 18 meses.

2 todo el cobra o cal –cobra (para California) ha

sido usado o el plan es terminado totalmente por el empleo.

3   usted no es eligible para otro plan de grupo medico o medicare, (medi-cal en California).

4   usted no perdio su cobertura porque usted no hizp pagos

Si esta situacion ocurre, y usted califica hay una ventana de 63 dias para introducir una aplicacion por un hecho garantizado. HIPAA poliza de aseguranza medica. Usted necesitara obtener un certificado of cobertura de su cargador de seguro anterior. Este certificado puede ser usado como prueba de sus 18 meses de cobertura.

La porcion de contabilidad de el acto de HIPAA esta disenada a guiar a los proevedores de cuidado medico y proveedores de aseguranza en el manipulo de informacion personal.

Las guias y regulaciones son mucho mas estrictas que cuando el acto fue pasado y usted tiene mas control de como su informacion personal puede ser usada.

Programa de salud para familias

Hay otro programa ofrecido en casi todods los estados que permite a los padres obtener cobertura medica, dental y vision para los ninos. en California es llamado The Healthy families program. Es para padres que hacen mucho para calificar por ayuda publica. Pero no suficiente como para pagar por seguro medico para sus ninos. Para la website de California y mas informacion , www.healthyfamilies.ca.gov Casi todos los estados tienen un programa similar.

Capítulo 3

Aseguranza dental

Aseguranza dental es probablemente la mas mal entendida de el plan basico de aseguranzas. Casi todas las personas creen el plan es malo porque cuesta mucho y paga poquito. Vamos a ver las basicas de como la aseguranza dental funciona.

Nuestra compania ficticia, Tom's dental insurance, es formada para vender aseguranza dental en grupos. Los duenos quieren proveer un plan de beneficios que ellos puedan vender a un costo bajo que ayude a sus clients y hacer ganancias para la compania. Es muy importante que ellos hagan esta ganancia pues asi ellos pueden mantener su negocio. En su forma mas simple el plan de negocios require que los clientes hagan un pago mensual por el plan. Este pago es entonces usado para pagar dentistas,cargos de compania y ganancias.

La tienda de herramientas de david compra un plan dental para sus 100 empleados. El plan cuesta 5 dolares por semana por empleado por un total de $26,000 por ano. Cincuenta porciento de los empleados usan el plan a un pago mas o menos de $500 por un total costo de gastos de el plan dental de $25,000. Esto deja a la aseguranza de tom con $1000 por el ano para pagar sobrecargos y contribuir a ganancias. Este ejemplo ensena solo mitad de los empleados usando el plan... y solo $500 en beneficio! Este plan puede que tenga una subida de precio al renovarlo.

Planes dentales tipicamente tienen un porcentage alto de empleados que usan el plan comparado con otros programas de beneficios. Esto quiere decir que hay menos de los costos pagados que son alcanzables para pagar beneficios. Asi que el pago maximo que se paga es mas bajo, tipicamente $1000, $1500, o $2000 por mes. En michos casos

Planes dentales son voluntarios. Empleados que solo requieren limpieza anual casi no toman la aseguranza y rebajan el numero de pagos necesitados para cubrir aquellos que requieren mas trabajo. Tomando unos minutos para examiner, la effectividad de costo de el plan es muy bien recompensada.

Ahora vamos a ver los planes tipicos que hay. Los cuatro planes mas populares son DMO,PPO,EPP, Y Indemnidad. Todos los planes tienen algo en comun. Los planes coleccionan pagos de el cliente y pagan a el proveedor dental por servicios. Todos los planes negocian con el proveedor dental para asegurar descuentos por servicios en cambio a acceso a los clientes de el plan, la diferencia esta en que y cuanto el plan paga.

DMO

El plan de DMO es el plan de la organizacion dental de mantenimiento es muy similar a el plan de HMO usado para cubrir gastos medicos. El proveedor dental que accepte este plan es pagado una cifra especifica cada mes por el plan dental por cada cliente asignado a esa oficina dental. En cambio por esto el proveedor dental a acordado a dar algunos servicios por no costo adicional, y han acordado a descuentos especificos de el costo (co-pago) por otros servicios. Cada persona escogiendo este plan va a tener que escoger un dentista o oficina dental en particular que accepte este plan. Entonces este es su dentista primario. La intencion es que usted se quedara con este dentista por el tiempo de el plan y el es responsable por su trabajo dental.

El dentista primario es escogido de un grupo de dentistas que acuerdan a co-pagos por todos sus servicios. Estos co-pagos son ensenados en el acuerdo de cobertura que le da el proveedor de aseguranza dental. Cuando trabajo intensivo es necesitado un sumario escrito de procedimientos y cobros debe ser requerido antes de acordar a el trabajo.

Esta lista puede ser revisada con el acuerdo de cobertura. Si hay algunos desacuerdos, siempre haga preguntas antes de que los procedimientos dentales sean hechos. Si el procedimiento no esta en la lista de su aseguranza usted puede insistir en un procedimiento similar. Que si esta en la lista y va a ser cubierto a el costo acordado.

El dentista primario lo referira a un especialista cuando sea necesario. Casi todos los planes le permitiran cambiar proveedores cuantas vecesal mes si usted no esta satisfecho con su seleccion. Casi no hay limite a el numero de procedimientos que le pueden hacer porque cada procedimiento tiene su propio co-pago si usted va a un dentista fuera de la cadena usted no tiene cobertura.

PPO

La cadena dental de PPO esta organizada muy similar a la cadena medica PPO usualmente hay un deductible y entonces un porcentage el paciente tiene que pagar. Los planes son usualmente establecidos en tres formas, preventtivo, basico y mayor.

El preventivo incluye limpieza normal,rayos x, y examinaciones. Esto es usualmente permitido una o dos veces por ano sin o con poco cargo. Es en veces referido a un 100%beneficios,en la mayoria de los planes el deducible (tipicamente $50 o $100) no se aplica a procedimientos preventivos

El basico incluye mas que todo extracciones, rellenos, y servicios normales menos costosos. Algunas veces el trabajo pare canales en las raices y servicios perodental.son cubiertos en planes basicos y en otros planes son cubiertos como trabajo mayor. El deducible debe ser satisfecho primero y entonces un percentage es aplicado. Tipicamente el paciente pagara 10%,20$ o 30$ con la aseguranza pagando lo que resta.

El mayor incluye los procedimientos mas costosos como dentaduras, parciales y procedimientos cirurgicos. Trabajos mayors asi como en el basico en el cual el deductible debe ser pagado primero y entonces un percentage es aplicado. El paciente puede esperar pagar 40%, 50%. O 60% y la aseguranza paga el resto.

Planes de PPO siempre tienen un cobro maximo que el cargador de aseguranza pagara cada ano por cado persona asegurada en el plan. Ese cobro es tipicamente $1000 a $2500. Cuando usted se sale de cadena el plan PPO dental trabaja exactamente como el plan medico PPO. Su deducible y porcentage de co-pago usualmente va a ser mas alto . Usted tambien va a ser responsable de negociar un cobro igual a el UCR o lista de cobros o usted va a tener que pagar la diferencia. Muchos planes PPO tiene maximos mas bajos que ellos pagan fuera de la cadena. Con trabajos mayores en cualquier plan usted debe pedir en escrito el costo de los servicios que el dentista le va a proveer junto con costos suyos antes de que empieze el tratamiento asi no van a ver sorpresas ni malentendimientos.

EPO

El plan dental de EPO trabaja como el plan PPO dental excepto no hay beneficios fuera de la cadena. Por esta razon los pagos de el plan EPO son usualmente menos caros. Esto puede ser una ventaja considerando aue las cadenas de PPO y EPO son usualmente muy grandes comparada a las cadenas de HMO asi que hay una oportunidad major de encontrar el dentista que usted prefiere.

Indemmidad

Planes dentales de indemnidad trabajan como los planes de PPO excepto no hay cadenas para controlar los precios. Usted puede escoger cualquier dentista que desee aceptar el plan de seguro. Es muy importante aqui que usted se comunique con su dentista y cual va a ser la parte que usted va a pagar.si no usted puede recibir una sorpresa no muy agradable.

Capítulo 4

Vision

Hay dos tipos principales de aseguranza de vision. Uno es un plan de seguro que paga una porcion de los gastos. El otro es servicios descontados por medio de una cadena de doctores y clinicas de optomologia. El plan de seguros tipicamente va a ser mas caro y paga mas beneficios. El plan de servicios descontado va a haber negociado adentoo de la cadena por precios especificos y servicios en especifico. Si hay necesidad de lentes cualquiera de los planes le economizara dinero. Si lentes no son requeridos, y usted solo quiere el examen gratis, usted estaria major no pagando el costo y usar ese dinero para pagar un examen anual. Siempre busque a el costo vs el servicio que usted va a recibir.

El plan tipico de vision PPO tiene un examen de vision gratis entre su cobertura o un deductible

especifico hacia el examen de vista. Usualmente $10 a
$25 por el examen.

Usualmente es permitida una cantidad por marcos de
lentes igual a una calidad de marcos . estos usualmente
no tiene costo para el paciente. Los marcos mas caros
requieren que usted pague la diferencia.

Lo mismo es por los lentes. Cierto tipo de lentes
son cubiertos y extras son usualmente pagados por
el paciente. Casi todos los planes cubren un costo
especifico hacia los lentes de contacto.

Siempre hay limites de tiempo por cada servicio.
Tipicamente usted es permitido un examen anual o
cada dos anos. Lentes son permitidos anualmente o
cada dos anos.y marcos son permitidos anualmente
o cada dos anos. Un plan tipico permite un examen
de vista annual, lentes anualmente, y marcos cado
dos anos. Los planes de tiempo mas corto son mas
costosos.

Hay algunos planes que solo cubren el gasto de
articulos para la vista y no el examen. Esto puede ser
bueno si su plan medico permite un examen anual de
vista.

Capítulo 5

Pre-Tax vs Post Tax

A ntes de los anos medios de los setenta casi todas las companias grandes que proveian beneficios de aseguranza de salud pagaban el costo total. Esta era la era en que el alto costo de servicios medicos empezaron a ser un tema mayor y las companies empezarona cambiar algunos de sus costos a los empleados. En 1978, las regulaciones de el IRS empezaron a entrar en efecto. Estas regulaciones permitian a el empleado que estaba pagando una porcion de su costo por cobertura medica por medio de deducciones de su pago a hacer que estan deduciones fuesen echas antes de sus taxes, permitiendo asi que el empleado usase dolares antes de deducciones para pagar por algunos beneficios. El programa reducio la cantidad de el sueldo y creo una ganancia para el empleado y el empleo. A traves de los anos , la idea de pre –taxing beneficios se ha vuelto lo normal, y el programa inicial crecio a incluir planes flexibles par costos medicos y cuidado diario de dependientes. Nosotros veremos esto mas tarde en el capitulo.

Cobros pre-taxing pueden ser usados para la porcion de el empleado medica, dental y el plan visual. asi como planes suplementales. Come seguro de cancer, enfermedades criticas y costos de hospitals. Algunas companies recomiendan guardar los pagos de pre-taxing para planes de disability y algunas companies recomiendan no pre-taxing, disabilidad, enfermedades criticas u otros planes con pagos en cantidad grande. Esta diferencia entre la variedad de los planes viene de la interpretacion de los codigos de el IRS. Y el hecho que casi nunca sabemos que es lo que el IRS va a hacer el proximo ano.con seguro de vida por ejemplo, usted co esta permitido pre-tax el costo para mas informacion acerca de esto y que es lo que el IRS permite o no permitem usted puede ir a la website de el IRS www. irs.gov y lea acerca de la seccion 125 y todos sus anectodas.

Para major entender los beneficios de pre-taxing beneficios de aseguranza, nosotros necesitamos hacer una simple arithmetica. Empezemos con un hombre que tiene un income de $30,000 por ano. El esta en un calculo de 20% y paga $200 por mes por beneficios medicos. La siguiente tabla muestra el efecto que esto tiene en lo que el lleva a casa cuando los beneficios son pagados con post-tax o pre-tax .

	POST TAX		PRE-TAX
Monthly income	2500		2500
tax@20%	500		
pre-tax costo			
de beneficios	200		200
net pay /pago neto	1800	pagp neto	2300
		tax@20%	460
Take home pay	1800		1840

Como podemos ver, la columna de post-tax ensena los taxes y beneficios restados de el pago . Lo que el empleado se lleva a casa es $1800. en la columna de el pre-tax podemos ver que los beneficios son restados primero y taxes son qutados de el salario de la cuenta mas baja. Esto permite un tax-bill mas bajo y proviene unos $40 por mes mas para recibir en su salario. Esta diferencia es donde el termino "taxsavings" fue fundado. El beneficio de gastar pre-tax dolares por beneficios crea un efecto de reunir taxes y sube el pago que se lleva a casa.

En este momento es importante poner emphasis que el ahorro derivado de los beneficios de pre-taxing vienen de ahorros de tax. Si usted no esta pagando taxes , no hay beneficio. Algunos con un income de familia de $20000 por ejemplo y cuatro dependientes probablemente no tendra un bill de tax. Pero seria una Buena idea de pre-tax planes medico, dental y vision. Porque usted recibira un pequeno ahorro en su cheque durante el ano . planes de reembolsos medicos y planes de cuidado de dependientes no tienen valor de ahorro de tax.

Usted tambien tiene que ver a el efecto de el largo plazo de pre-taxing. Una nota de cuidado es usualmente incluida en el pre-tax plan para advertir que pre-taxing beneficios van a reducer su income y puede que reduzca su seguro sociall beneficios. Aun cuando esto es verdad la perdida es reganada a medida de el tiempo

Otra area de preocupacion en el pre-taxing es pagos de disabilidad al contrario de los otros beneficios discutidos aqui los beneficios de disabilidad se vuelven income taxable cuando los pagos son hechos pre-tax Su empleo tiene que pagar FICA taxes por los beneficios que usted recibe, lo cual causa una deduccion en sus beneficios y puede causar problemas con su empleo. El monto ahorrado por pre-taxing es bueno si usted nunca tiene un reclamo pero cuando un reclamo es hecho el ahorro rapidamente se esfuma.

Porque entonces algunos vendedores de disability recomiendan pre-taxing Ellos estan entrenados a ensenar ahorros de tax como una manea para reducir ls costos de los beneficios. Y como casi nosotros no necesitamos aplicar por disability, este ahorro reducira el costo.

Usted necesita cuidarse de pagos grandes cance, enfermedades criticas y planes de Puente medico. Para cuando este libro sea publicado los planes de beneficios pagados bajo estos planes siguen siendo non taxables. Pero bajo reglas que el IRS ha usado en casos similares, esto puede cambiar en cualquier momento. Asegurese de obtener las ultimas reglas de el IRS de parte de el representante de la compania de seguros en el momento de compra. Si ellos no tienen esa informacion entonces es mas prudente a no pre-tax.

Yo recomiendo que usted nunca pre-tax planes de disabilidad. Yo recomiendo que usted haga pre-tax a planes medicos, dental y vision, y casi otros productos voluntarios.

Cuentas Gastivas Flexibles

Una cuenta gastiva flexible es otra manera de ahorrar tax dolares. Esta cuenta trabaja permitiendo que usted ahorre dinero en una cuenta separada. Los fondos van a ser gastados despues en costos medicos y gastos de costos de dependientes. los ahorros son realizados haciendo que el empleo reduzca pago maximo de el empleado antes de los impuestos ser calculados para el total que va a ser depositado en estas cuentas. Este programa da a el empleado un ingreso mas bajo que paga impuesto y resulta en un gasto mas alto de ingreso.

Cuentas de reembolso medico

Planes de eembolso medico son los mas frequentemente usados de cuentas flexibles gastivas. Un plan de reembolso medico permite que el empleado ahorre dolares de pre-tax. Para pagar fuera de bolsillo gastos aprovados, como el co-pago y deductibles, recetas medicas, chiropractico, cuidado de la vista, y otros medicinas sin receta medica. Hay una lista de gastos aprovados con cada cuenta. Asegurese que usted tiene acceso a esta lista antes de escoger su plan. La cantidad que usted puede seleccionar es un total por ano y no puede ser cambiado sin un cambio social de familia. Matrimonio, divorcio, nacimiento o muerte de un miembro de la familia. O un cambio mayor de parte de su trabajo para el empleado o su esposa. El IRS pone las barreras, pero interpretacion les da un poquito de lugar a los planes individuales. Cualquier fondo en esta cuenta al final de el plan annual puede ser perdido, asi que es importante que usted sea conservativo al escoger el saldo que va a ser apartado. El empleo pone el minimo y maximo que los empleados pueden apartar.

La mecanca de como un plan de reembolso medico funciona puede ser confuso para la persona que esta considerando usar esta cuenta por la primera vez. Aunque no todos los planes funcionan igual, hay mucha consistencias. Vamos a ver un plan tipico.

Nuestro empleo escoge este plan $1200 es el gasto que ella quiere ahorrar por el plan annual. Ella escogio esta cantidad estimando lo que gastaria fuera de su bolsillo por gastos aprovados durante el ano. Ella sabe que puede que gaste mas o menos, asi que $1200 es un calculo estimado.

Co-pado y deducibles	$500
Dental	500
Vision	200
Prescription	200
Total	$1400

Otra consideracion es el "usalo o pierdelo" regla. El IRS requiere que cualquier dinero que sobre al final de el plan de ano es perdido. Nota esta no es una regla de las companies. Es una regulacion de IRS. Su calculo, entonces debe ser conservative. Esta bien si usted no tiene mucho en a cuenta. Si este es el caso, usted paga com ousted normalmente pagaria co su pago de cheque normal. Pero si usted tiene mucho en la cuenta, usted lo puede perder

El $1200 es deducido de el cheque de el empleado y dividido igualmente por el ano. Si hay veinte y cuatro periodos de pago, $50 son deducido de cada cheque. La mayoria de los empleos tiene un tercer administrador de el plan. (TPA) para administrar estas cuentas y disponer de los fondos. Los empleados tienen acceso a los fondos hasta el maximo que haya puesto desde el primer dia. Si el empleado en nuestro ejemplo gasta todo los $1200 en enero y el TPA reembolsa el total de $1200.no hay dinero en la cuenta para gastos durante el resto de el plan anual. Puede haber confusion pues esta es una cueta de ahorro, no es deducciones de aseguranza y depositos a la cuenta contina por el resto de el plan anual para reembolsar la cantidad gastada en enero.

Para tener acceso a los $1200 el empleado tiene que tener gastos aprovados. Un par de recetas de lentes puede ser un gasto aprovado. Si el gasto fuera de su bolsillo es $120. el empleado puede pagarlo y obtener un recibo de el optometista y entonces entregarlo a el TPA y es reembolsado por los $120. Casi todos los TPA envian el cheque entre cuarenta y ocho horas de recibir un reclamo. (contando el tiempo por correo, esto quiere decir usted recibira su cheque en una semana a diez dias.) Los $120 son substraidos de la cuenta de el empleado dejando $1080 hasta el proximo reclamo.

Cuentas de cuidado de dependientes

Cuentas de cuidado de dependientes ayudan con el gasto de cuidado de ninos asi el empleado/o esposa, pueda trabajar. Cuidado de dependiente puede ser cuidado de dia, gastos de despues de la escuela para ninos menores de trece anos, o cuidado para adultos dependientes. El empleado puede guardar hasta $5000 por ano en la cuenta de cuidado de dependiente. (o $2500 por ano si los esposos estan reclamando retornos de impuestos por separado.) Este lan tiene la misma regla de "usalo o pierdelo" asi que es importante ser conservative y acertado cuando calcule su gasto projectado. Si el ingreso de familia de el empleado es $25.000 o menos el credito por cuidado de dependiente puede ser una opcion mejor. Hay una formula que le ensena cual es la major opcion. Casi todas las companias que ofrecen este programa proviene una pagina de inscripcion para determiner si el plan de cuidados de dependientes o el credito de impuesto es major. Si el ingreso de su fmilia es menos que $25.000 anualmente o usted tiene mas de dos ninos en cuidado de dependiente, asegurese de usar la pagina proporsionada.

Si usted escoge este plan, usted asigna una suma para ser apartada. Esta suma es deducida de su cheque durante el ano no como el plan medico de reembolso, usted solo puede usar el dinero que esta en su cuenta. Usted paga el gasto de cuidado de el dependiente como usual. Y despues de que los servicios han sido proveidos, usted entrega su forma de reclamo y sus recibos a el TPA, quien le enviara el cheque de reembolso.

Capítulo 6

Seguro de disabilidad

Seguro de disabilidad (DI) es probablemente el mas mal entendido de todos los planes que son proporcionados en un paquete de beneficios. En este capitulo yo tratare de definir los typos differentes de DI. Y darles suficiente informacion para que usted escoga el plan que es major para usted.

DI es casi siempre llamado "proteccion de pago," "reemplaze de pagos" o un termino similar que envuelve los beneficios a el sueldo. Se asume que si usted se disabilita usted no tendra un sueldo. Los beneficios de este pla le permiten que usted continue a cuidar de sus responsabilidades financieras durante el periodo que usted esta desabilitado. Y no teniendo un sueldo.

El tipico corto plazo disabilidad(en veces llamado (STD) plan paga un percentage de su sueldo de 5 a 60 porciento despues que usted este fuera de su trabajo de cero a treinta dias por un periodo de tres meses a dos anos. Como usted puede ver. Hay mucho lugar para variacion entre planes

El tipico largo plazo disabilidad (algunas veces llamado LTD) plan, pagara un percentage de su sueldo de 25 a 70 orciento despues de que usted este fuera de trabajo de treinta dias a un ano. Y pagara de cubic abis a edad sesebta y cinco o mas, otra vez hay mucho lugar para variacion.

Por la gran variedad de planes, hay tambien una gran variedad en precios que usted paga por los planes individuales. Pero el precio no es el unico factor Para escoger un plan que sea bueno para usted, usted debe examiner todo el plan. Aqui hay una lista de las partes de el plan DI.

Premium
Edad
Periodo de eliminacion
Costo de pagos de beneficio
Tiempo de pagos de beneficios
Regla de condiciones pre-existentes
Que constituye disabilidad
Que condiciones hay para no ser cubierto

Esto no quiere decir que usted no debe ver los premiums. Vea el costo de el plan en una base anual. Plan A por ejemplo, le cuesta $50 por mes o $600 por ano.Y paga un beneficio de $500 por mes despues que usted ha estado fuera de trabajo por dos semanas por un ano. Usted tendria que estar sin trabajo por siete semanas para colectar tanto como lo que usted guardo, esto es cuando usted ve a su vida y su estilo de vida y hace un a decision educada de la probabilidad de usar DI. Una persona joven que no es muy activa puede estar mejor .ahorrando dos meses de sueldo para emergencies, asi como cualquiera que maneje una motocicleta debe estar sin covertura de accidente.

Su edad tambien afecta los premiums. Csi todos los planes tienen precios altos por edad alta. Yo no creo que el riesgo es mayor, pero yo se que como envejecemos, nuestras reacciones son un poquito mas lentas y nuestras heridas tardan mas en cicatrizer Es intelgente reviser las causulas de la edad. Tambien averigue a que edad el plan para de pagar beneficios. Casi todos los planes lo cubre de edad dieciocho a sesenta y cinco, aunque algunos van mas si usted sigue trabajando.

El periodo de eliminacion es el tiempo usualmente demostrado en dias. Despues que su disabilidad empieza antes de que su covertura empieze. Planes de corto plazo tipicamente son de cero a treinta dias, aunque algunos planes llegan hasta sesenta dias o noventa dias este es el periodo cuando usted esta solo, el plan no esta pagando sus beneficios. Como escoge? La pregunta simple y examen es "cuanto tiempo yo puedo estar sin my sueldo?"

Cuando considere un plan de DI, tome en cuenta todos las otras posibles Fuentes de ingreso. Rhode Island, new jersey, newyork, Hawaii, california , and Puerto rico ofrecen un plan de disabilidad de el estado. (SDI que va a ser discutido mas adelante), usted tambien puede tener pago de enfermo, plan de vacacion, pago de empleo con plan de continuacion con salario, ahorros o hasta parientes con buen Corazon que lo ayudaran. Lo mas que usted pase solo antes de que los beneficios comienzen a pagar va a hacer pagos mas bajos cuando comience a pagar.

Largo plazo DI tipicamente tiene un periodo de eliminacion de tres, seis, o doc emeses. Esta designado a sobre tomar despues de corto plazo disabilidad. Y cuando otras Fuentes de ingreso se vencen

La cantidad de su pago de beneficios es usualmente expresada como un porcentage de su pago normal y este puede variar de veinte y cinco a setenta porciento. El plan de disabilidad de corto plazo tipicamente no coordina con otras Fuentes de ingreso incluyendo otros planes de DI, asi que los beneficios son pagados encima de SDI y cualquier otro ingreso. Los percentages estan hechos de manera que se le paga algo cerca de su sueldo sin sobre pasarlo. El plan SDI de California tipicamente paga 55% de su sueldo, un veinte y cinco o cuarenta porciento DI plan suplemental es ofrecido. En estados sin el programa SDI el percentage es usualmente de sesenta a ochenta porciento. Companies de seguro y empleos tratab de vugukar ek percentage muy cerca asi ellos no le dan una razon para regresar a el trabajo.

Es importante recorder que planes DI son afectados por planes pre-taxing sis u compania hace pr-tax a el premium, su beneficio se hace ingresos taxable. Asegurese de mantener esto en mente cuando cuando considere cuantos beneficios usted necesita. Casi todos los planes le permitiran sacar menos que el maximo beneficio permitido. Por ejemplo, si 40 porciento de su ingreso es $2000 pero por otras Fuentes usted puede sobre pasarla con $1200, recibiendo la cifra menor le ahorrara dolares en sus premiums. Pero si el plan es un plan de pre-tax y sus beneficios son con impuestos usted puede necesitar o escoger $1500 para obtener el mismo ingreso para llevar a casa.

Planes tienen diferentes duraciones de pagos de

beneficios. una duracion es el periodo de tiempo el plan paga cuando usted esta fuera de trabajo. El tipico DI corto plazo plan varia entre tres meses a dos anos, usualmente seis o doc emeses. Si usted sufre una fractura de pierna y esta fuera de trabajo por siete meses. El plan de seis meses le pagara beneficios por seis de sus siete meses. El plan de doce meses pagara los siete meses completos., pero el premium por el plan de doce meses va a ser mas caro.

Largo termino DI es disenado para empezar despues de el termino corto de DI se ha expirado y tipicamente paga por cinco anos, hasta la edad de sesenta y cinco , o hasta el retiro. Largo termino plan de DI son tipicamente pagados por su empleo y tienen un periodo de eliminacion mas largo, cual puede ser seis meses. A un ano. Casi todos los planes tambien coordinan con otras coverturas de disability usted pueda tener. Coordinacion quiere decir que la compania de DI no pagara mas que 100 porciento de los beneficios declarados. Cuando usted presenta un reclamo, la compania de seguros preguntara si usted tiene otras covertures. Ellos entonces reduciran su covertura para coordinar con su otras covertras.

Esto puede hacerse confuso cuando su empleo ofrece un plan de termino largo que paga beneficios despues de un periodo de eliminacion de seis meses. Su empleo puede tambien ofrecer un plan de SDI voluntario, asi usted puede escoger covertura que pagara un beneficio por seis o doc emeses. El plan de corto termino reclama los beneficios debidos y no cordina con ninguna otra covertura y paga encima de ninguna otra fuente usted pueda recibir. Esto es probablemente cierto. Casi todods los planes de SDI no son coordinados.

La cordinacion viene de el plan de largo plazo. En el ejemplo abajo usted puede ver como este funciona. Su largo plazo plan (LTD) ofrece un beneficio de 70 porciento. Y el plan de plazo corto (SDI) ofrece un beneficio de 60 porciento. El periodo de disabilidad es dieciocho meses. El plan de corto plazo paga 60 porciento por el primer ano, y entonces ae cancela. Despues de seis meses cuando usted aplica por largo plazo disabilidad, la compania de aseguranza le preguntara si hay alguna otra covertura. Como el plan de corto plazo esta pagando 60 porciento por los primeros seis meses de el periodo de covertura de el plan de largo plazo, el plan de largo plazo solo pagara 10 porciento, lo cual es la diferencia entre el 60 porciento que el plan de corto plazo paga y el 70 porciento ofrecido por el plan de largo plazo. Cuando el plan de corto plazo para de pagar despues de un ano, entonces el plan de largo lazo mpieza a pagar el 70 porciento.

Fijese en la siguientes figuras de tiempo.

Time	0meses	6meses	12meses	18 meses
STD@ 60%	-----------------------------------			
LTD@ 10%		------------		
LTD@ 70%			---------------------	

Usted recibira 60 porciento por los primeros seis meses.de su plan de corto plazo. Usted va a recibir 70 porciento po los proximos seis meses, con su plan de corto plazo pagando 60 porciento y el plan de largo plazo pagando 10% usted recibira 70% por sus ultimos seis meses de disabilidad. Con el plan de largo plazo pagando el 70 porciento completo.

Cuando usted tiene planes multiples, es muy importante que usted entienda las reglas de coordinacion de las diferentes companies de seguro. Si alguien le dice que ellos no necesitan explicar cordinacion, o por alguna otra razon usted decide no informar a la compania de aseguranza de largo plazo acerca de su plan de corto plazo considere esta nota de cuidado. Cuando un reclamo es acompletado uno de las formas que usted firma es que la forma esta llenada completamente y verdaderamente por lo major de su sabimiento. Si hay un no en una caja donde debe haber un si, y la compania de seguros averigua, ellos pueden considerar un fraude y negarse a aceptar su reclamo. Algunos LTD planes no cordinan con algunos STD planes. Asegurese usted entiende la regla de cordinacion de las todas las companias involucradas

Condiciones pr-existentes son una parte de todos los planes de disabilidad. Palabras tipicamente usadas suenan asi.

Beneficios no van a ser pagados por los
primeros doce meses despues
De el dia de entrega por ninguna condicion
que fue diagnosticada, tratada, o discutida
por cualquier professional medico durante los
doc emeses antes de el dia que fue entregado.

Cada plan tiene su manera de escribir esta clausula. Algunos planes tendran largo o corto periodos, y algunos haran la pre-existente condicion permanente. El punto es que la compania de seguro no tenga que pagar por un accidente o enfermedad que ocurrio antes de que usted fuese cubierto. Esto tambien puede ser aplicado a reclamos de maternidad. Algunos planes no pagan beneficios de maternidad si el nacimiento es dentro de los primeros nueve meses despues de el dia que la poliza fue entregada. Asegurese de leer y entender las condiciones pre-existentes clausulas antes de firmar la aplicacion.

Algunas veces una poliza de DI son entregadas con reglas garantizadas. Esto uiere decir que usted esta garantizado y que la poliza va a cumplir si usted cumple los terminus de la garantia. Esto usualmente elimina todos o casi todos las preguntas de salud en las aplicaciones. Pero usualmente no elimina las clausulas de las condiciones pre-existentes. Cuando a usted le dicen que la poliza esta garantiada, usted todavia debe reviser por condiciones pre-existentes.

Cada DI plan tiene descripciones que explican disabilidad. Esta es la condicion usted deber satisfacer en orden para la compania de seguros pagar beneficios por su reclamo. Una tipica descripcion es " la inabilidad de ejecutar last tareas normales de su trabajo" hay muchas vriaciones de estas descripciones, casi todas requeriran el certificado de un medico o otra persona calificada medicamente y debe ser entregada con el reporte de reclamo.

Todos los planes tienen una seccion que explica que no es cubierto. Estas son usualmente llamadas "exclusions" Exclusiones casi siempre estan incluidas en la poliza, pero tambien estan anotadas en el folleto. Fijese en la escritura mas pequena. Usted encontrara un dicho asi.

Esta poliza no pagara si el reclamo es un
resultado de Guerra o molestias civiles El echo

de un acto illegal, participacion de cualquier
forma de carreras
Exibiciones organizadade carreras, ser piloto o
miembro de un equipo
En una linea aerea, o colgar en paracaidas o
nrincar en bungee.

Exclusions pueden ser mas o menos detalladas;
algunos planes excluyen deportes de bachillerato en
las escuelas si usted cubre dependientes. Diferentes
companias de seguro tienen preocupaciones por lo que
es determinado peligroso, asi que lea esta seccion de
la polza o folleto cuidadosamente.

Seguro de disabilidad de el estado

Considere una nota rapida para aquellos on plan
de disabilidad de el estado. Este es un plan que paga
un beneficio de disabilidad si usted esta enfermo o se
lastima en el empleo.el plan de California paga 55%
de su sueldo despues que usted esta fuera de trabajo
por siete dias y continuara pagando hasta un ano. Si
usted esta en uno de los seis estado con este tipo de
programa usted necesita saber que estos beneficios son
considerados cuando usted esta permitido escoger un
plan de disabilidad voluntario. Por eso es que con casi
todas las companies de aseguranzas de disabilidad en
estos estados, usted no puede obtener mas de un 40%
de beneficios.

Seguro de vida

Muchas companies provienen una cantidad modesta de seguro de vida para sus empleados. Usualmente un beneficio neto de $10,000, $20,000 o mas. Algunas companies ofrecen un multiple de salario, como una o dos veces su salario annual. Muchas companias estan reconociendo que empleados qieren mas seguro de vida y estan empezando a ofecer opciones voluntaries adicionales.

El beneficio de seguro de vida, cual es pagado cuando se muere el asegurado nombrado en la poliza (usualmente usted) es comprado para cuidar a sus sobrevivientes. Siempre y cuando hay muchas otras formas que explican como la aseguranza de vida es mejor para usted yo ofrezco una simple y conservativa manera de examinar sus necesidades.

Tosdos mecesitamos suficientes fondos para cubrir gastos finales para que no sean un peso para nuestros familiars, amistades o el estado. En estos dias , si usted no tiene $10,000 en valores netos, usted necesita esa cantidad de aseguranza por lo menos. Casi todas las aseguranzas pagodas por el empleado no son portable, cual quiere decir si usted cambia trabajos o lo deja, usted pierde ese beneficio. Yo recomiendo que usted cargue este minimo $10,000 en adicion a cualquier aseguranza temporaria que su empleo pueda tener. Para una persona soltera sin responsabilidades esto puede ser lo unico que necesita.

Para una persona que esta casada y tiene familia, las reglas cambian. Todos tenemos suenos y deseos para nuestras vidas y las de la familia. La manera en que esos suenos y deseos lleguen a florecer es definida por el ingreso que usted produzca cuando este vivo. Cuando ese ingreso para, entonces su seguro de vida se convierte en su ingreso. Que es lo que va a suceder para dares cuenta de el sueno de su familia?.

Para entender seguro de vida nosotros tenemos que mirar como es construido. En este libro estamos viendo solo a seguro de vida como es comunmente proveido en sus beneficios de empleado. Los tres tipos usted va a ver mas seguidos son Term, universal,y whole life.(termino, universal y vida completa). Una manera simple de ver la diferencia entre los tres es viendo a el valor que pagan. Seguro de termino de vida no tiene pagos de valor. Piense como si fuese aseguranza de carro ---no choque, no dinero. Seguro de vida universal es un tipo de seguro mas permanente donde usted paga un saldo mas alto u la compana de seguro la cual paga intereses en el premium de una tarifa flotadora que se afinca en el Mercado. Seguro de vida completa es un seguro permanente en donde usted paga un premium mas alto y la compania de seguro paga una tarifa fija en el premium.

Cuando las companies de seguro deciden vender aseguranzas. Hay unas cosas basicas que elos ven. Nosotros tenemos que recordar estas companias estan en negocios para hacer ganancias, El dicho de la mission de una compania puede dictar otras metas, pero sin ganacias ellos no se mantendran en su negocio.para hacer ganancias ellos tenen que conseguir mas dinero por medio de premiums y investimientos, que lo que ellos pagan en reclamos y gastos de operacion. Como consumidores nosotros tenemos que recordar este concepto basico asi como estudiamos los precios.

Cobros de premiums normalmente son basados en edad, fumador y una variedad de preguntas de salud, asi como en veces genero. Casi todos los planes de seguro ofrecidos por medio de planes de beneficio de empleados son planes unisexo, asi que no hablaremos de genero como base de cobros. Los mejores precios van a las personas jovenes que no es fumador y pueda contester las preguntas de salud en una manera positive. Esto es porque la historia ha ensenado que esta persona vivira mas tiempo y pagara mas premium que la persona mayor, el fumador, o alguien con problemas de salud.

Una de las ventajas de obtener su seguro de vida por medio de el plan de beneficio de su compania es el concepto de garantia. Esto quiere decir que usted tendra una garantia que la poliza va a ser entregada si usted cumple las condiciones de la garantia. Algunos planes ofrecen asuntos de garantias o garantia modifica en la primera oportunidad que tengas de comprar la aseguranza de vida. Esto es cuando usted es empleado o cuando el empleo ofrece introduce el plan por primera vez. Usted va a ser cobrado en vase de sue dad y estado de fumador o no, pero las preguntas de salud van a ser mas simples y en veces borradas por complete. Esta es una estrategia de el Mercado. La meta de la compania de seguros es vender mas polizas. El volumen elevado de ventas cubrira la perdida potencial causada por un pequeno grupo de compradors de poliza que es cubierto pero no hubiese sido aceptado si se le hubiese hecho las preguntas medicas. Esto es bueno par alas companies de seguro. Es tambien bueno para el empleado que tome ventaja de la oportunidad

Seguro de vida de termino

Termino es la forma mas simple de seguros de vida. El plan basico de termino es un especifico costo de beneficios de seguro que se le paga a la hora de la muerte de la persona que esta asegurada y esta en efecto por un tiempo en especifico. Un plan de termino de 10 anos por $100,000 es bueno por 10 anos. Al final de los diez anos esa poliza es terminada. Usted no obtiene dinero de regreso. Su beneficio es tener el uso de la aseguranza de vida por el termino de diez anos a un costo bajo. Al final de el termino usted puede que tenga el derecho de renovar por otro periodo a un costo mas alto comparado con su edad corriente.

Si un empleo ofrece un plan basico de seguro de vida para todos sus empleados, es generalmente un plan de termino de grupo. El termino es el periodo que dura su empleo con la compania, y estos planes usualmente no son portables o sea transferidos, asi que cuando su empleo termina tambien termina su plan de seguro No hay excepciones, asi que asegurese de reviser su guia de beneficios o preguntarle a su representante de beneficios.

Casi todos estos planes son convertibles, no confunda convertible con portable. Portable quiere decir que usted puede continuar el plan, como esta escrito, despues que usted termina su termino de empleoy a el mismo precio que usted o su empleo estaban pagando cuando usted estaba empleado. Convertible quiere decir que usted puede continuar el plan despues que usted termina su termino de empleo, pero usted tiene que convertir la poliza a otra forma, asi como vida completa y pagar un premium mas alto. Esto es usualmente una Buena idea solo si hay problemas de salud previniendolo de obtener otros seguros de viday la clausula de convertirse no require un escrito de salud nuevo.

La forma mas comun de seguros de termino de grupo voluntario es el temino de cinco anos. El premium de este plan es calculado en base de cinco anos, usualmente veinte,veinteycinco,treinta, treintaycinco,etc. esto significa que el premium o pago que usted hace esta basado en su edad en el momento que usted compra la poliza o cuando la poliza es iniciada. El ano en que su edad pase uno de los bandos su premium subira a el proximo nivel y se quedara asi por los proximos cinco anos. Hasta que usted llegue a la edad de cuarenta, lo que sube es minimo, pero a los cuarenta ycinco y mas, los pagos en premiums pueden ser significantes. Si usted tiene este tipo de plan, tenga cuidado de cuanto los pagos suben cada vez que usted pasa a un uevo bando de edad.

Seguro de terminus es una Buena decision si usted es menor de cincuenta, en Buena salud, necesita sobre $100,000 en covertura y solo nesecita la covertura por un periodo de tiempo en especifico. Mantenga esto en mente: un tipo de seguro de vida no es mejor que otro. Usted necesita determinar cuanta aseguranza de vida usted realmente necesita, porque la necesita y cuanto usted puede invertir. Despues les dare unos ejemplos de clientes con diferentes necesidades y la major manera de satisfacer estas necesidades.

Seguro de vida universal

seguro de vida universal es casi siempre llamado seguro "permanente" no como seguro de termino, universal se queda enforzado siempre que los pagos de el seguro son pagados. El costo de aseguranza es el costo que la compania de seguro cobra para mantener la aseguranza enforzada. El premium pr aseguranza de vida universal consiste de el costo de seguro mas un costo adicional que cuando invertido por la compania de seguro, proveera por el costo alto de seguros a medida que usted envejece. Este dinero adicional crea el valor de dinero en efectivo de la poliza. El dinero en efectivo le permite pagar un premium nivelado por la vida de la poliza. Recuerde, que el costo de aseguranza sube cada ano que usted envejece, no como el seguro de termino, en el cual los premiums suben cda ano, o cinco anos o cuando la banda de edad lo requiera, y la poliza termina al final de el termino. Con seguro universal de vida, el costo de premium es constante y la poliza continua. El costo extra que es pagado a el premium es lo que paga para que esto suceda.

Si universal es mas cara, cual es el valor de comprarla?niversal va a ser permanente y portable. Usted va a poder mantener esta poliza hasta que muera, aun cuando cambia empleos. Casi todas las companies le permitiran mantener su deduccion de pago de el plan de seguro de vida universal, a el mismo costo, si usted cambia trabajo o se retira. Esto es una ventaja especialmente si usted desarolla problemas de salud a medida que envejece. En la mayoria de los casos el precio se mantiene constante, y en casi todos los planes, a menos que halla una baja en los intereses, su premium esta disenado a hacer que la poliza dure hasta que uste llegue a los noventa y cinco anos (in casi todos los casos 100anos).

Para una persona joven viendo a el plan largo, el plan universal puede ser el de major valor. Vea el ejemplo en la tabla siguiente. No como polizas individuales, casitodos los planes vendidos en el Mercado de los beneficios de empleados tienen tarifas unisexo. Asi que las tarifas van a ser igual para homnre y mujer. El factor principal va a ser fumador o su edad. Una persona que esta comprando una poliza de $100,000de vida a la edad de veinte y cinco y que no es fumador pagara los siguientes premiums por 30 anos.

Tipo	$ por semana	anos de premium	total pagado	valor
Termino	$ 4.60	10	$2.392.00	$ -
Termino	$ 6.38	10	$3.317.00	$ -
Termino	$16.06	10	$12.526.00	$ -
Total		30	$18,235.00	
Universal		30	$20.077.00	$ 34,729.00

Aseguranza de vida de termino es mas barata, aun con la subidas de precios requeridas por las edades de los empleados. Sin embargo recuerde que la poliza termina cuando usted llega edad cincuenta y cinco y no hay mas covertura. Esto es usted gasta $19,431 con no otro regreso excepto la seguridad realizada de saber que usted fue cubierto por treinta anos. Con universal usted gasta casi $2.000 mas sobre treinta anos, pero usted tiene una poliza continua, a el mismo costo y valor en efectivo con la garantia de cuatro porciento por sobre $34,000. los resultados son diferentes si usted tiene una edad diferente o es fumador. Lo mas Viejo que usted sea cuando usted empiece, lo menos que le regresan sin embargo el precio sigue constante y la poliza se mantiene permanente.

Mantenga en mente que estos son exemplos de cobros dados para ayudarlo a entender que preguntas tiene que hacer acerca de diferentes polizas. Una no es mejor que la otra! Los planes tienen diferentes propositos. Algunas personas compran seguro de termino y invercionan la diferencia en costos de premiums para un retorno major a traves de el tiempo. De las miles de personas con quien he hablado de este tema, he conocido muy pocas que actualmente hicieron el nvestimento. Yo prefiero creer que el mejor valor de universal es su permanencia. Cuando usted llega a una edad que el premium de el termino se hace imposible, todavia esta universal continuando a el mismo premium que usted estaba pagando cuando usted primero se registro. Termino entonces es para un especifico periodo de tiempo, sin embargo universal es permanente por vida.

Aqui hay algunas cosas ofrecidas por aseguranza de vida universal. Hay otras y no todos los planes ofrecen estas. Si hay alguna cosa que usted no entiende asegurese de preguntar.

Muerte acelerada
Esto le da la opcion de recibir un porcentage de el beneficio de muerte, usualmente 50 a 75 porciento, sei a usted le diagnostican con una enfermedad terminal y es es supuesto que morira dentro de un ano.

Muerte por accidente
Este es seguro adicional que paga si su muerte es causada por un accidente. Usualmente hace su monto de beneficio doble.

Termino adicional para esposa o hijos
Este le permite agregar seguro para un miembro de familia para que sea parte de su poliza. Numeros son usualmente limitados pero el costo es bajo.

Desden de el premium
Este quita todas las deducciones mensuales si disabilidad total ocurre antes de que llegue a la edad de sesenta y cinco. Algunos planes requieren permanente disabilidad aunque otros quitan las deducciones mientras usted esta desabilitado. Usted puede continuar pagos despues de que la disabilidad termina.

Beneficios aumentados
Este le permitira a la compania de seguro subir su beneficio de aseguranza en el costo que uno o dos dolares por semana comprara for cinco o diez

anos sin ninguna evidencia de no aseguranza. Esto le da a usted una manera facil de aumentar sus beneficios sobre el tiempo con un pequeno aumento cada ano,en vez de pagar un premium mas alto en el principio.

Seguro suplementario de salud

Cobertura supplemental de salud se ha vuelto muy popular como una manera de ayudar con los gastos relacionados a una enfermedad en especifico o un accidente. El costo de seguro medico sigue subiendo, y cortes en beneficios o aumentos en los deducibles y co-pagos estan empezando a ser retenidos para el aumento de el precio. Esto causa que usted tenga que pagar costos de su bolsillo. Otra forma popular de casi todas las polizas suplementarias es que los beneficios son pagados en efectivo, y usted puede usar este dinero para cualquier cosa. Por ejemplo, su seguro desalud puede cubrir el doctor y hospital gastos. Pero no paga su alquiler o gastos de cuidado de ninos.

Encima de asistir con co-pagos y deduccibles, cobertura supplemental puede ser usada para pagar a enfermeros o gastos de el hogar. Puede asistir con su ingreso de disabilidad o ayudarlo a acompletar otros gastos inesperados. Los planes mas populares de beneficios suplementales son los planes de acidentes, seguro de cancer, y cobertura de enfermedades criticas, ingresos de hospitaly planes de Puente medicos.

Planes de accidents

Planes de accidente son probablemente los mas populares de los beneficios suplementales, estos bienen en muchas formas con diferentes ideas. Algunos tienen corto plazo disabilidad que pagara un beneficio de DI por mes encima de el beneficio de accidente. Algunos planes ofrecen cobertura para esposas y dependientes. Otros ofrecen beneficios opcionales para disabilidad o hospitalizacion debido a un accidente. Porque este es un plan favorito universal, es importante dde asegurarse que usted entiende cuales son las cosas que el plan que su compania ofrece tiene.

El plan basico de accidente esta disenado a ofrecer predeterminados beneficios por heridas causadas por accidents. Este dinero es usualmente en adicion a cualquier otro beneficio pagado por la aseguranza medica o otro plan. Es pagado a usted no a los doctores o hospitals y puede ser usado para cualquier cosa. Un plan tipico ofrece pagos de beneficios por las siguientes necesidades.

Ambulancia
Aparatos
Sangre
Quemaduras
Dislocacion
Tratamiento en emergencia

Herida de vista
Fracturas
Desgarre de rodilla
Cortadas

La mayoria de los planes ofrecen pagos de beneficios por mas cosas de las que yo puse en la lista, pero esta lista le da una idea de como el plan funciona. Por ejemplo diga que usted tuvo un accidente de motocicleta y sufre dos ruptures en su pierna derecha, este plan le pagara asi:

Ambulancia	$100
Cuarto de emergencia	$150
Aparatos (refuerzo)	$100
Rupture en hueso de pierna (1)	$1200
Rupture de hueso de pierna (2)	$600
Entrada al hospital	$750
Diez dias en hospital	$2000
Total	$4500

Usted recibira unos $4500 adicionales para asistir con co-pagos, deducibles, o cualquier otro gasto que pueda ocurrir.

Exclusiones tipicas son Guerra, volando como piloto o miembro de el equipo, deportes profesionales, participacion en un crimen de felonia, estar intoxicado, y participar en carreras. Si selecciona el plan de ninos, algunos planes excluyen futbol de bachillerato y otros deportes. Asegurese reviser exclusions en el plan ofrecido.

Seguro de cancer

Seguro de cancer es ofrecido por el alto riesgo de cancer hoy dia. La asociacion Americana de cancer dice que el hombre tiene uno en dos riesgos por vida de desarollar cancer. Y las mujeres tienen un riesgo en tres. la asociacion de ACS tambien dice que los cinco anos de sobrebimiento de personas que han tenido proyecciones de cancer es 80%. Ellos tambien dicen en la edicion 2000 de hechos y figures de cancer que si todos los americanos participaran en prevencion de cancer, este calculo subiria a 95%. (footnote cancer facts and figures, American cancer society,2000)

Usando las figures de la sociedad de cancer, costos directos cubiertos por la mayoria de planes medico serian 35%. El costo indirecto de 65% que usted [aga incluye perdida de ingresos, viajes a centros de tratamientos estaduria, comidas, co-pago y deducibles, segundas opinions, y buscando tratamiento fuera de su cadena medica.

Viendo las estatisticas de ACS, no es sorprendente que seguro adicional para cancer se ha hecho tan popular. Muchas companies differentes ofrecen planes de seguro de cancer, los cuales son un pago de beneficio singular o un plan de indemmidad que paga beneficios dependiendo en lo que ocurra.

Los dos tipos de seguros de cancer tienen generalmente definiciones generales de cancer y limitaciones. Todas las companies de seguro tienen sus propios escritos, asi que asegurese de revisar la definicion de el plan que es ofrecido por su empleo. Cancer es usualmente definido como una enfermedad caracterizada por los incontrolables y abnormales crecimientos y desparcimiento de celulas invasivas malignas. Esto puede incluir melanoma, hodgkin's y leukemia. El cancer tiene que ser diagnosticado clinicamente o patologicamente.

Todos los tipos de seguros de cancer tambien usualmente incluyen un beneficio de mejoramiento. Este es un beneficio que paga una vez al ano para que usted tome un examen de prevencion de cancer. La suma pagada varia, pero es usualmente entre $50y $150. los examenes cubiertos por diferentes companies no son todos iguales, pero ususalmente incluyen mamographia, PSA para cancer de la prostate, rayos x del pecho, biopsia para cancer de la piel, colonscopy, hemocultura analisis de eces, y flexible sigmoidoscopia diferentes polizas pueden cubrir diferentes examenes de cancer, asi que assegurese de revisar su poliza para determinarcual examen es cubierto. Cancer no maligno es usualmente cubierto a un precio mas bajo que los canceres malignos.

Casi siempre hay un periodo de espera entre entrega de poliza y dia que se efectua. Esto quiere decir que si el cancer es descubierto entre este periodo, (ususalmente treinta dias, pero puede ser mas largo) no va a ser cubierto. Para estar a salvo siempre espere que el periodo de espera termine antes de tomar cualquier examen. Otra limitacion comun es la clausula de condiciones pre-existente, que casi siempre dice que si usted ya ha tenido cancer o tiene canceres de la piel, usted puede que no sea elegible para covertura. Casi todos los planes tendran diferentes limitaciones. Algunos planes dicen "nunca ha tenido" y otros los aceptaran si usted esta considerado en remission o curado por diez anos, aunque otros puede que sea cinco anos, y aun menos para cancer de la piel. Es muy importante de revisar cual regal el plan que su empleo ofrece tiene.

El beneficio de pago singular es un plan que permite que usted escoja un pago singular, usualmente entre $5,000 y $50,000, para ser pagado cuando lo diagnostican. El costo de este plan es usualmente basado en la edad, fumador y el costo escogido por el beneficio.

El plan de indemmidad es mas complicado y puede incluir beneficios de tratamientos, beneficios de paciente,, transportacion, y alojamientos beneficios, beneficio de cuidado extendido y otros. Casi todos los planes tienen un folleto que describe los beneficios individuales. Aqui hay unos ejemplos de los beneficios ofrecidos.

Estadia de hospital	$200 por dia
Visita a el doctor	$20 por dia
Ambulancia	$150 por viaje
Radiacion//chemoterapia	$10,000 por ano
Tratamiento experimental	$10,000 por ano

Este dinero puede ser usado para cualquier cosa. Siempre revise su folleto para saber que es lo que su plan paga.

Seguro de enfermedades criticas

Aseguranza de enfermedades criticas en veces llamada seguro de sobreviviente, esta disenado para personas que obtienen una de las nombradas enfermedades criticas y sobrevive. Estas enfermedades estan conocidas por el alto costo de tratamiento y tiempo perdido de trabajo, lo cual normalmente pone a el sobreviviente en muchas deudas financieras.

Un plan tipico cubre ataque de Corazon, stroke, dano de un rinon, organos transplantey cirugia de arteria de bypass coronario. Algunos planes cubren mas enfermedades otros menos. Revise el plan de su empleo paraver cual enfermedad cubre y cual no.el plan tipico permite escoger un nivel de beneficios de $5,000 a $50,000 para ser pagado cuando le de el diagnostico inicial. Estos planes usualmente tienen un periodo de espera y exclusions para condiciones pre-existentes.

Planes de ingreso de hospital

Planes de ingresos de hospital estan disenados a cubrir co-pagos, deducibles, y otros gastos que puedan ocurrir cuando usted esta hospitalizado. El plan tipico pagan una suma por dia por cada dia que usted esta hospitalizado. Este monto es normalmente uno a uno y medio a dos veces de el costo basico por dias pasados en cuidado intensivo. El valor de este plan es que llena cualquier cosa que haya en su otro plan medico. Por ejemplo, sis u otro plan medico es PPOcon un 80/20 pago y el costo de hospital por dia es $1000, entonces un plan de $200 por dia pagara el 20% de su responsabilidad.

Planes de Puente medico

Estos planes estan disenados a llenar la diferencia que se encuentra en el deductible inicial de muchos planes medicos. Estos cortan gastos y pelean aumentos en premiums con deduccibles elevados y co-pagos. El plan de ingresos de el hospital ayuda con co-pagos y deducibles, el plan de Puente medico hace lo mismo, pero en una manera diferente. Este plan es normalmente hecho en niveles de beneficios de $500 a $5000 a ser pagados en admicion a un hospital. Si su plan medico tiene un co-pago o deducible de $500, $1000 o mas cuando lo admitan al hospital, este plan le recobrara su dinero en efectivo fuera de bolsillo que usted gasta no importa cual plan medico usted tenga, pero es mucho mas util si su plan tiene vacios que necesitan ser llenados.

Planes de cuidado de largo termino

Planes de cuidado de largo termino no son usualmente incluidos en los beneficios los empleados y son usualmente vendidos por separados algunos empleos ofrecen un lugar en su cheque cuando la union y asociaciones respaldan estos planes. Algunas aseguranzas de vida tanbien han empezado a incluir ofertas que ayudan a pagar gastos de cuidado de largo termino.

Cuidado de termino largo (LTC) se refiere a hogares de cuidado y enveces gastos de cuidado en casa. La mayoria de las companies usan la criteria de actividades de siete dias, vistiendose, comiendo, transferiendose, usando el bano, banandose, transportandose uno mismo y tomando medicinas---para determinar cuando usted califica por pagos. Usted no debe de poder efectuar dos o tres de estas actividades, para calificar diferentes planes tienen diferentesrequisitos.

El plan tipico va a ser hecho para pagar un supuesto

beneficio por cada mes por cada cuidado de largo termino hasta un maximoen tiempo o dolares. Un plan puede ofrecer $4000 por mes por vida, hasta un maximo de $240,000. lo amplios y los beneficios hacen que este sea un plan indiviluadizado.

El plan de largo termino de cuidado es usualmente encontrado en los planes de beneficios de el empleo y es un plan pegado a el plan universal. Como es cargado es facil de entender, asi que es mas popular en grupos. Con este plan, un empleado puede comprar uan poliza de $1000,000 de vida universal. Una ventaja de la poliza o de ser cargado, dira que si cuidado de largo termino es necesitado antes de morir, el beneficio de la poliza (o una porcion de el beneficio) puede ser usado para pagar estos gastos. Tipicamente esto quiere decir que la poliza pagara $100,000 dividido por veinteycinco meses, lo cual es $4000 por mes por veinteycinco meses. Algunas variaciones de esto pueden permitir $2000 por mes por cincuenta meses, a el nivel de $4000. cualquier quiera que sea el monto de beneficio no usado por cuidado de largo termino va a ser dejado para el beneficio de muerte. La excepcion a esto es si la extension fue comprada, el dinero que sobra sera entonces aplicado sola hacia el costo original de el beneficio.

Planes de grupos legales

Aunque son muy populares a los planes de empleados, casi la mayoria de los planes de grupos legales no son aseguranzas. Pero planes para cortar el costo de servicios legales. Ellos funcionan como un plan de salud de HMO usted paga un pago mensual, escoge un abogado o una oficina, y recibe servicios legales por bajo o no co-pagos. Hay dos basicos tipos acceso y comprensivo. Un plan de acceso cuesta como $150 por ano y proviene un simple testamento y acceso a el telefono para advertencies legales y simple servicios de un abogado.

Un plan comprensivo cuesta $300 por ano y cubre negociaciones, testamentos, tratos o contratos. Algunos planes provienen consulta legal en casos criminales hasta un limite de costo. Despues de el cual el abogado continuara representando por un costo reducido. El abogado normalmente no maneja los casos que envuelven a usted y su empleo, o toman un caso ya en progreso. El mayor beneficio es la facilidad de tener acceso a un abogado.

Algunas veces esto puede prevenir que las cosas se salga fuera de lugar y que resukten en algo mayor, y una demanda ma s cara.

Hay muchos planes . asegurese de leer los folletos asegurese de los servicios y y cualquier otro costo mas alla de su premium.

Capítulo 9

Así que ahora que hago?

La pregunta mayor es cuanto cuest la aseguranza y porque es tan cara. Peiodicos y articulos de magazines han sacrificado arboles en la foresta explorando y contestando estas preguntas. La pregunta major es como puede usted tener un dfecto directo en sus costos de salud. Primero, no fume, beba, sobrecoma,o poco cma o coma las comidad erradas. No haga nada peligroso y ejercite regularmente. No se acerque a personas enfermas, obtenga revision medica cada ano, y obtenga sus vacunas. Practique moderacion. Evite actividades que obviamente se sabe van a causar enfermedades y trate de vivir una vida llena de salud. Mas importante, recuerde que no importa que bien vivimosnuestras vidas, siempre Habra veces que vamos a necesitar attencion medica.

Asi que pregunte que plan es bueno para mi? con planes de beneficios de compania usted no siempre va a tener opciones en que plan escoger, con companies pequenas, usted puede que tennga uno o dos opciones. Antes de ver los beneficios, determine que tipo de covertura usted tiene. Es usted soltero sin responsabilidades? Tiene usted una familia que necesita ser protegida? Se esta usted acercando al retiro y ya tiene lo necesitado para una vida comoda? O apenas esta empezando y todavia esta colgando ? todos somos diferentes. Aqui hay tres basicas guias. Yo he desarollado a traves de los anos. Estas puede que no sean perfectas para todos, pero es una Buena guia para empezar.

1. No sea una carga para otros. Todos necesitamos seguro medico.nohay manera o garantia que usted no se enfermara o lastimara. Alguien siempre tiene que pagar las cuentas.
2. todos necesitamos poder pagar nuestros gastos de sepelio. Todos moriremos nada mas no sabemos cuando, alguien tendra que pagar las cuentas.
3. Si usted tiene familia, usted necesita proveer por sus beneficios, si usted esta Enfermo o lastimado y no puede trabajar, o si usted muere y los deja sin Ingresos.

Un buen argumento puede ser hecho para justificar la necesidad de cada planen el plan de beneficio que su empleo ofrece. Por eso ellos estan alli. Para decidir que planes son Buenos para usted, yo sugiero un metodo que considera riesgo y costo. Usted trata de cubrir el riesgo mas grande por el menos costo. La historia muestra que el riesgo mas grandes que usted se enferme, se lastime o muera. Estas opciones crean gastos de cuidado de salud y pueden parar su ingresos. Yo sugiero que su prioridad debe ser seguro medico, la aseguranza de disabilidad, y entonces seguro de vida.

Considere su edad, historia de salud de familia su propia historia de salud que tan activo es usted? Usted maneja mucho? Es usted fumador? Usted toma? Que riesgos usted piensa usted tiene? Cuanto de el costo total su seguro de salud pagara? , estas consideraciones pueden llevarlo a el plan supplemental que es bueno para usted. No dos personas son iguales. Usted necesita escoger el major paquete o cobertura que funcione para usted a el mejor precio que usted pueda pagar.